Move with a Purpose: Addressing Common Behavior Issues on the Autism Spectrum Before They Grow Out of Control

Bobby Newman, PhD, BCBA-D

Dana Reinecke, PhD, BCBA-D

ISBN: 1466488336
ISBN-13: 978-1466488335

Dedication

This book is dedicated to Dr. Gerald ("Jerry") L. Shook, Ph.D., BCBA-D, Founder and retired CEO of the Behavior Analyst Certification Board.

Jerry, on behalf of all families who love someone with a developmental disability, thank you for always advocating so hard for our families. This book is a tribute to your dedication to our families and the consumer. Your vision and all you sacrificed created a credential now protecting our most vulnerable population, nationally and internationally. You are our worldwide ABA Superhero!

With much love and admiration

–Jennica Nill

Cover Design

Our thanks once again to Ken and Sharon Braun of Lounge Lizard Worldwide for our book cover conception and creation. You can contact Lounge Lizard at:

Lounge Lizard Worldwide, Inc.

620 Johnson Ave., Suite 1B

Bohemia, NY 11716

Telephone (631) 581-1000, Fax (631) 563-6278

For a description of their innovative marketing and public relations services, visit www.Loungelizard.com

Additional thanks to Patrick Bardsley for taking the cover photo.

CONTENTS

Introduction

There are certain behaviors that are more commonly displayed by individuals diagnosed on the autism spectrum than by typically developing individuals. Some common examples include particular speech patterns (e.g., echolalia or use of third person language) or ritualistic behavior such as always performing tasks in the exact same manner and becoming upset if asked to vary in any way.

Such behavior may remain stable without intervention, or may actually grow and become a life-altering problem. Rarely will this kind of behavior resolve on its own. To take one example from my clinical past, one student insisted on carrying a toy train in each hand. By the time he was brought to me for help, he was insisting on holding 50 trains in his arms at nearly all times. He was unable to engage in any other behavior due to his arms being loaded down, and would become physically aggressive if anyone attempted to have him put the trains down or if he could not find all his trains, in just the order in which he left them.

The key point of this volume is that while such behaviors may be more common among individuals diagnosed on the autism spectrum, such behavior need not be accepted as unvarying and allowed to take over the individual's life. With proper intervention, these troublesome patterns can be eliminated or at least brought to typical levels and thereby no longer interfere with the person's functioning. While we have striven to keep a comparatively light and conversational tone in the current volume, as we have done in previous works, this is not to take away from the fact that the stakes we are playing for are frighteningly high. Addressing such behavioral issues successfully can mean the difference between independent and supervised living, to highlight just one stark reality among many.

Each chapter in this book will provide an example of a common difficulty, as well as a means of addressing that difficulty. We must always, however, keep in mind the basics of Applied Behavior Analysis (ABA) and remember that there are no shortcuts. As I put it in a previous work, anyone who wants to tell you that they can give you a treatment plan for your child without first conducting a functional analysis/assessment is selling something. The factors maintaining behavior in each individual case must be thoroughly investigated so that we can tailor-make a treatment plan for that behavior by that individual.

That being said, what follows are examples of common scenarios and treatment methodologies that have proven successful in the past. We hope it will provide some background and clues to guide your efforts.

Bobby Newman, Ph.D., BCBA-D

Chapter One

Don't Say it if You Aren't Going to Do it!

Bobby and David Newman

For our first discussion, we are going to address the general area of compliance with spoken instructions. We are deliberately going to start off with an example that is universal, and not particular to the autism spectrum. A later chapter will provide more in-depth discussion. Consider this a "warm up" to begin thinking behaviorally.

To set the scene, it was a really nice summer afternoon. David and I were at the refreshment stand at the beach near our home, following a very satisfying round of bodysurfing. There's nothing better than a refreshment stand lunch and ice cream after some bodysurfing with someone you love, I hope we can all agree. That is, unless you're sharing the refreshment stand with the people we were sharing it with.

There were two adults and four kids on the table platform with us. The children seemed to range in age from about three to about seven. They were engaged in a variety of behaviors, including yelling at each other and at nothing in particular, tattling on each other for saying dirty words, running around and climbing on and jumping off the tables, and stripping off their clothing (including their bathing suits). The adult response was to angrily call out to the children and threaten that they would not get ice cream if they did not settle down. The adults continued to chat among themselves as they ordered the ice cream. You can guess what the children were doing. Their behavior had not changed, and neither the children nor the adults in this group seemed particularly happy. The adults seemed to have given up on attempting to establish or maintain order or even safety, and the ice cream supply never really did seem to be in question.

I asked David if he would like to eat our stuff at the tables or back at our towels. He quickly opted for the towels. As we walked away, he said to me in his philosophical nine year old voice, "Well, *that* was unpleasant!" I could only agree.

We can easily identify the two key problems. The first is that the adults were working from a "what are you losing rather than what are you earning" stance. This stance is generally tricky, as it leads to issues of just "how bad" do you need to be in order to lose the item in question. To be successful, behavioral consequences must never be arbitrary. Criteria must be established beforehand.

The second problem is also obvious and more fundamental. The adults in this case were making threats that they obviously did not intend to keep. This is the first rule of good relationships and behavior management, and the kiss of death if you break it: "DON'T SAY IT IF YOU AREN'T GOING TO DO IT!"

Forgive the textual shouting, but this simple statement cannot be emphasized enough. How many times have you heard a parent say "Ok, we're leaving this place because you are . . . " and they are still there 30 minutes later? You've probably seen it more times than you can count. Effective behavior management is about having predictable interactions and consequences. Anything that undermines that predictability undermines the whole system. Promising (or threatening) a particular consequence and then not providing it reduces credibility. You would never promise a reward you weren't prepared to offer, would you? Taking it away from simple behavior management, if you offered someone a job for a particular rate of pay, would you then refuse to pay if the person did the job correctly? Of course not, because you would know that the person would not believe you in the future and would no longer work under your supervision and would probably advise others to avoid you as well.

Why should the rules be any different when we are talking about interactions with our children? Of course, the obvious answer is that they shouldn't. Yet, just take a listen at the local supermarket, park or playground. We all hear people threatening to do everything from taking away activities or treats through putting people through walls! Of course we hope that no one would ever do that last one, but what about the ones before? Let's consider:

1. A behavioral rule has been established and agreed to by all.
2. A consequence if that behavioral rule is broken is established.
3. That behavioral rule is broken.
4. If the established consequence is not provided, for example not buying the ice cream from the earlier example, what is the incentive to follow the rules?

It is most important, therefore, to think before you speak. Are you truly prepared to carry through on the behavioral rules that you are establishing? If you aren't, don't establish the rules that way! Once again, don't say it if you aren't going to do it. Even if you mean well, even if someone truly is sorry for what they have done, established consequences should be carried through. Changing rules because you feel badly about following through, or because the child feels badly about what (s)he did, doesn't help. In fact, it only undermines the system when we change rules midstream and leads to confusion all around. That being said, there is never a reason to hold a grudge. When an agreed upon rule is broken and an agreed upon consequence is delivered, then the situation is done. We move on and get right back into our mutually reinforcing relations.

To see this in action in a simple teaching scenario, look at a common discrete trial teaching interaction. A teacher says "touch your head." If the student touches his/her head, a reinforcer is delivered. If the student touches the wrong body part, or does not touch his head within a pre-set amount of time, the teacher might provide a gentle physical guide to prompt the behavior and then the task is attempted again.

Consider also a common behavior treatment issue. A five year old student diagnosed with autism has dropped to the ground as an avoidance or escape behavior. A staff member directs the individual to stand up. If the student does not stand up, what should be done? Should the staff member repeat him/herself? As we sometimes joke, this puts the staff member in the role of an unarmed police officer: "Stop . . . or I shall say stop again!"

But no, the rules should not change. Provided we have established that the student is not dropping to the ground in order to obtain physical contact with staff as a reinforcer, we would do as we would do in the discrete trial teaching scenario described above. If the student complied with instructions, we would reinforce. If the student did not comply, we would provide gentle physical guidance to help the student to comply. In this way, (s)he would learn that we expect instructions to be followed the first time they were provided. To return to the general theme of this volume, it is true that students diagnosed on the autism spectrum may have language or social skill deficits that make such challenging behavior more likely. Whether the behavior will continue to be displayed or not, however, depends largely upon how the behavior is addressed.

Never give instructions if you aren't prepared to carry through. Don't say it if you aren't going to do it.

Chapter Two

Stop Overanalyzing the Behavior

Sheila M. Jodlowski

As parents, we sometimes attach inaccurate meaning to behaviors. We do this for a number of reasons, but mostly because it provides an excuse for why our child's behavior is occurring. Having an excuse—valid or not—somehow makes us feel better as parents. An excuse tells us that our child isn't just a bad kid, and that we are not bad parents. It establishes that there is a reason why our child is doing this to us, and if we can just address that reason then everything will be okay. Except it's not. Our child continues to engage in undesired behavior and we continue to strengthen the bond between the behaviors and the excuses.

Providing excuses for behaviors doesn't solve the problem by changing the behavior. It might make us feel better that we have given a reason as to why the behavior is happening. It might even let us save face in front of others by having that excuse handy to be able to brush public outbursts aside—"He's having a hard day" or "He's tired." Yet, the excuse does not make the behavior go away. No matter how many times it is said, or how elaborate the excuse, the behavior will persist. We need to address the behavior itself, not the excuse, not the emotion behind the excuse, and not the child. We must address the behavior.

A parent came into my office very concerned and clearly distressed. She was convinced that her two-year-old was expressing her anger over remaining in a crib. When I asked why she had that impression, she told me how her daughter was removing her feces from her diaper and smearing all over the crib. The mother would then go into her room and have to bathe the girl and change the whole crib. The mother, being a professor of developmental psychology, was certain that this was her daughter's way of telling her that she was angry that she was still in a crib and her brother was in a "big bed." The mother was surprised by my response, "I think she's telling us she's ready to be potty-trained."

It turns out that the mother was not ready to tackle potty-training at that point, but note that we did take a different perspective when looking at this behavior. We discovered that it was more fun for the child to get mom to come into the room and give her a bath than it was to hang out in an empty crib. A few toys left in the crib allowed the child to play until mom could come in to get her out of the crib. The child was not angry. She was not resentful. She was just bored, and she figured out that this particular behavior got mom's attention really quickly and then she had the additional engagement with mom during the bath.

Behaviors happen for a reason. As parents, we often attach our own emotional feelings to the behaviors of our children—looking for the validation of the reason the behavior occurred. We don't need to look for validation. We need to look at how the behavior works for the child. When we examine behaviors that way, looking at what happens as a result of the behavior, we get a clear picture of why it's happening.

Recently another mother called the office very distressed and I could hear her child screaming in the background. She told me she was not bringing her 6 year old to his session that afternoon. She felt that 2 sessions a week were clearly just too much for him to handle and this was his way of letting her know. He would not go to the car and had been screaming for an hour about not wanting to go. This child was no longer attending school because of inappropriate and aggressive behaviors seen there. He had practically no reading skills, very few writing skills, below grade level math skills, speech delays, and significant delays in social development. It was difficult for him to sustain eye contact for any length of time, and it was challenging to get him to remain on task for more than 2 minutes. With a great deal of reinforcement and direct instruction, he was progressing during his individual sessions (2 hours long), but it was still hard work for him. The alternative to working on learning tasks that were difficult for him was sitting on the couch and watching TV. Given the choice, which would he want to engage in? And perhaps if he engaged in behavior that had historically been very successful for him (removal from school, removal from class during difficult work) he would not have to participate in a challenging activity.

This was the case for this child. He engaged in inappropriate and aggressive behaviors and did not have to attend sessions as a result. His behavior was successful. He was not being asked to do what was difficult for him. He preferred to sit on the couch rather than do something that was not as much fun, and work avoidance and TV watching were the result of his behavior.

Applied behavior analysis has taught us to examine behaviors within the environment in which they occur. Behavior always occurs within a context, and it is that context that must be carefully examined to understand why the behavior is happening. Examining the behavior itself for clues to emotional validation will not yield answers as to why behavior is happening. It might make us feel better to attach some type of emotional reason to behavior: he's angry with me, she's expressing her resentment, it's too much for him; but these reasons, true or not, do not account for why the behavior happened. Only the environment: what happened before and after the behavior, is going to tell us why a behavior occurred. Examining this sequence of events is part of a functional behavior assessment.

The research on functional behavior assessment supports its efficacy as a behavior change tool. Once we discover how a behavior is working in the environment, we can then replace the behavior with a more appropriate alternative to meet the same end (Frea, Koegel, & Koegel, 1993). Carr and Durand (1985) documented the predictable relationships between behaviors and the environment in which they occur. They were able to show how some of the people in their study only engaged in problem behaviors when they were receiving very little attention. Others in the study only engaged in problem behavior when a difficult task was set before them. For each person, there was a different relationship between problem behavior and what was going on at the time in their environment. Research continues to show that finding the function of problem behavior, or answering the question, "How does engaging in this behavior change the environment for the person?" is the best way to reduce or eliminate problem behaviors (e.g., Hanley, Piazza, Fisher, & Maglieri, 2005; Iwata et al., 1994; Neef & Peterson, 2007)

Returning to our earlier example, we replaced the toddler's feces-smearing behavior with toys left in the crib with which she could play upon waking. When she woke and played with the toys, Mom would then enter and provide attention following this very different behavior. Mom's attention then reinforced the appropriate behavior rather than the inappropriate behavior. The child still got Mom's attention, but we changed the behavior which yielded that end result.

Likewise, the six year old who very cleverly figured out how to watch TV and eat cheese curls on his couch was able to undergo a behavior change when his parents changed their response to his negative behavior. The child was told he could have access to the television and a snack of his choice, but that was contingent upon completing his session. He was not lectured or otherwise scolded in any way. If he refused and began to engage in inappropriate behavior, his parents walked away and told him that was fine; he could do that if he wanted. As soon as he went to turn on the TV, parents blocked access to it and reminded him that he could watch TV as soon as his session was over, but otherwise he did not have access to it. The child missed one session. Each time after that, he immediately got into the car and went to his sessions as soon as his parents reminded him of the arrangement. The end result was the same for the child. He watched TV and ate a snack. The behaviors involved in reaching that end, however, had been changed by altering others' responses to inappropriate behavior. Once the contingencies for appropriate and negative behaviors had been altered, the child behaved as was most effective at achieving what he wanted.

It is easiest to accomplish this when we separate the child from the behavior. Your child is not using inappropriate behaviors to tell you anything about the manner in which you are parenting. Your child is not engaging in inappropriate behaviors because he is a bad kid. Behaviors should be viewed only as behaviors; they must be detached from the child. When we separate the behavior from the child we can more easily address just the behavior without our emotional attachment to the child interfering. We are not treating the child. We are treating the behavior. So just look at the behavior. How is the behavior making the environment work for the child? Is the child getting access to what he wants as a result of his behavior? Is the child getting to spend extra time with you? Even scolding and lectures can sometimes act as reinforcers because you are engaging with your child in an exchange.

Once we are looking at just a behavior, we can become more objective about how the child is using that particular behavior. What is happening when you see the problem behavior occur? Was anything asked of the child (e.g., "Do your homework")? Did they have to stop doing something preferred to do something less preferred (e.g., "Turn off the TV and go brush your teeth")? Did they lose access to attention (e.g., Mom got a phone call, or a friend is over to play with a sibling)?

Also ask yourself what's happening after the behavior occurs. Did the child not have to complete a task or the challenge was reduced (e.g., Dad helps with the homework, or the homework is sent back to school with a note explaining why it couldn't be completed)? Did the task get delayed for a significant amount of time (e.g., you tell him to brush 10 times before he finally does in a stomping, puffing show of anger)? Did the child gain access to attention quickly (e.g., Mom hangs up the phone because she cannot have a conversation and scolds the child, or Dad runs into the room because siblings are fighting over toys and he scolds the children)? Did the child gain access to what (s)he wanted (e.g., she got her pacifier because she was crying so much)?

The answers to these questions will help you to figure out the function of your child's problem behavior. Once you answer the questions, honestly, then you will be able to teach a replacement behavior. Replacement behaviors are new skills. They are taught.

Your child does not know them yet, so you must teach them. Have him gain access to preferred activities only through compliance and following directions. Teach your child to request attention by asking to be read to, or asking to watch a movie together. Augmentative communication may need to be taught to children who currently have limited spoken language. Help your child to go through the action of the task before expecting him to do it on his own. Look for the replacement behaviors that will have your child achieve the same end, but in an appropriate way.

Remember that children will behave in the way that is most effective for them. Look at their behavior simply, do not over analyze it or layer it with so much emotion that you can no longer see the behavior. Simply look at the behavior and what the child gains by acting that way. This will lead you to the true reasons for the occurrence of the behavior.

Chapter Three

Whining to Winning:

Making Your Home a No-Kvetch Zone

Melissa Slobin

"The kvetchatorium is closed!" This was the phrase coined by my Jewish mother in an attempt to "stop the whining" (*kvetching* is the Yiddish translation) between my two sisters and I during our early years. It never really worked. Instead, I thought she was from a far-away planet where they made up peculiar words like "kvetchatorium." Today, perhaps in a less creative style than my mother's, when my three girls whine, I tell them, "My brain does not process the way you're speaking right now." Spoken tongue-in-cheek, at least one daughter will reply, "What's wrong with mommy's brain?" The real answer here is nothing! The human brain is simply not equipped to hear whining tones as anything but irritating. Whining does not compute.

The What and Why of Whining

Whining consists of language presented in a characteristic structure: increased pitch, slow production and varied pitch contours when compared to other types of speech (Sokol, Webster, Thompson, & Stevens, 2005). Like nails on a chalkboard (now obsolete thanks to interactive whiteboards), a whining child can seriously challenge one's sanity. So why do our children whine? Is it to annoy us? To provide payback for all the whining we did to our mothers? Or are we teaching and reinforcing the behavior without realizing it?

In general, it appears that the function of whining behavior is to gain attention or to achieve a desired end (e.g., getting a cookie). For the purpose of this chapter, we will assume that your child's basic needs are being met and that he or she is not neglected or treated in a way that righteously warrants whining. In this case, let's assume the antecedent of whining is boredom. The task, therefore, will be to teach your child that whining will not result in the desired outcome.

Extinguishing Whiny Behavior

To eliminate this annoying behavior, the first step involves auditory discrimination of whining versus the target tone of voice. Perhaps the child is unaware of how the whining sounds. Without extensive mimicking or mockery, the negative effects of the sound of whining should be taught to the child. Through modeling or by recording and playing back the child's own whining, auditory feedback can be a helpful start to extinguish this behavior. Children need to learn that nobody wants to listen to whining because it is unpleasant to hear. They need to understand that this way of speaking is not acceptable.

If whining persists after the auditory discrimination task and modeling, put the behavior on "ignore mode" (don't reinforce the behavior, or "extinction" in what my colleague calls "behaviorspeak"). Refuse to talk with him until he corrects his tone of voice and expresses himself in what you have established to be an acceptable manner. Any type of recognition, whether it's giving in to what the child wants, or losing your cool and screaming at him, will reinforce the behavior and, thus, the whining will not stop. It may even escalate. Remember, a child looking for attention may accept negative attention as a final resort. Giving in to the child sends the message that the whining worked and, therefore, he will keep using this powerful skill to get his way. He must be reminded that using the target tone of voice will elicit a positive response but whining is an unproductive and exhausting exercise.

Teach Your Children

When struggling to address our children's whiny behavior, one must do a bit of self-reflecting to rule out the possibility that we are inadvertently teaching our children to whine! Ask yourself if you have truly broken your own childhood habit of whining. I certainly catch myself complaining about all of the tasks that need to get accomplished in a given day. One can argue that complaining is a form of whining. If the child is hearing you or your significant other or another adult role model whine, he or she is likely to acquire this behavior through social learning. Instead of moping or moaning about the things that didn't go right in *your* day, why not show your child that while nothing is perfect, you can deal with disappointment in a way that won't turn off the very people you're turning to for support. So remember, no kvetching!

Perhaps most importantly, remember to provide ample positive reinforcement when the child does not whine. This can be done in the form of verbal praise. For example, "I like the way you asked me that." You should also provide immediate attention to the child when appropriate requests/statements are made. He will learn that if he speaks in an appropriate and acceptable manner instead of whining, he will indeed get the attention he is seeking.

Helping the Child with Special Communication Needs

Regarding individuals with communication disorders, particularly individuals diagnosed with autism spectrum disorders, whining can take on an entirely different function. In addition to gaining attention, a child who is not effectively communicating his needs may whine due to profound frustration. If this is the case, it is essential to teach an appropriate mode of communication for this child. If he or she does not use speech production as a primary means of expression, speech-language therapy is warranted in order to teach the child an alternate way to communicate. The use of an augmentative-alternative communication (AAC) device should be evaluated as a functional means of communication. In fact, any system that utilizes tools, devices, symbols, pictures, words or gestures to compensate for communication deficits has the potential to decrease the frustration level and hence the whining (see Carr and Durand's work on functional equivalence, referenced elsewhere in this book, for example). A book of its own would be needed to address the special needs of children with communication disorders, but it is important to mention that almost all children can be provided with the communication tools they need to deal with their frustrations in a more appropriate and productive manner. It may just take an extra dose of patience and skill from your interdisciplinary team.

Pearls Before Whine: A No-Whine Checklist

So before the whining drives us to our wine cabinets—(bad joke), remember these key strategies:

- The behavior should not be reinforced if you want it to go away!
- Teach your child what the whining sounds like and make it clear that you will not respond to this manner of speech. *Ignore* the unwanted behavior.
- Keep your own whining and non-constructive complaining behavior in check.
- Positively reinforce the correct way of speaking with loads of praise and attention. You will eventually be able to bring it down a notch, but at the beginning you'll need to densely reinforce.
- For children with communication disorders, it is essential that you are working closely with a speech therapist to ensure an appropriate communication system for your child.

Be consistent and stay strong. You can conquer whining with these winning strategies. Congratulations. The kvetchatorium is now closed.

Chapter Four

You're Saying That Again!

Alayna T. Haberlin and Leigh Ann M. Shepherd

"Jordana, grab your jacket! It's almost time to leave for school!" Beatrice looks at her daughter as if today will be the miracle day that she will not hear, "I'm Peppa Pig (snort) and this is my brother George (snort, snort)," repeated through the last bit of their morning routine before heading out the door. Unfortunately, today is not that day, and lines from Peppa the Pig waft through the living room. Beatrice already knows that she is going to have to ask at least one or two more times before Jordana will get her jacket. "Honey, your jacket, it's in the kitchen!" Beatrice knows her daughter understands the words that she is saying, as this phrase has been a consistent part of their morning routine for many years. What seems to be the problem is that Beatrice just can't seem to find a way to get Jordana to stop repeating lines from her favorite TV shows or movies long enough so that Jordana can properly attend to what Beatrice is saying.

Jordana's "scripting" (repeating or "echolating" dialogue) of her favorite TV shows or movies is not only a problem at home, but has become even more problematic at school. Jordana's teacher, Mr. Larkins, has expressed his concern to Beatrice about Jordana's ability to follow teacher's instructions, disruption of the other students, and overall ability to learn while at school. One of his latest notes home stated that Jordana was saying, "Princess Fiona" over and over when she arrived to school. Mr. Larkins has a strict policy that he greets all the students that enter his class and that the students will reciprocate the greeting. Due to her scripting, it took about 10 minutes for Mr. Larkins to get a "hi" in response to his greeting on this particular morning. He expressed concern that this behavior would greatly interfere with Jordana's ability to learn and grow during the school year.

When we meet with parents or teachers, nearly all say that they want their child to be talking and interacting more with family members or classmates, typical areas of concern for caregivers of children with autism spectrum disorder (ASD). As the conversation goes on, however, and we begin talking about the child's vocal abilities, they will sometimes say something like, "My child is really good at nursery rhymes, he knows every Wiggles song by heart, and it is great that he is so musical, but do you think that you could get him to do it a little less? I really don't think I can handle hearing 'Big Red Car' one more time." Another common comment is, "Yes, the child in my class can talk when I ask her a direct question, but mostly she talks gibberish to herself with the occasional ear-piercing scream mixed in during the day. It would be nice if you could help her to stop this because it is disturbing the other students in my class."

One of the most challenging aspects of being a parent, caregiver, provider, or teacher for those diagnosed with ASD is deciding how best to reduce the amount of time the person diagnosed with ASD engages in stereotypic behaviors, often referred to as self-stimulatory behaviors or "stims." We should note at this point that we do not particularly like the terms "stim" or "self-stimulatory" *unless a functional analysis has demonstrated that the behavior serves that sensory feedback function*. Putting a label on the behavior doesn't explain it. We should only call it a self-stimulatory behavior if it has been shown to be an automatically reinforced response through a functional analysis/assessment. Otherwise, we might work on a behavior treatment plan assuming a self-stimulatory function when in fact there are other possible functions. We will present data later in this chapter from studies where precisely such functional analyses have been conducted.

Stereotypy is most often defined as repetitive movements or vocalization not seem to serve a purpose (Kennedy, Meyer, Knowles, & Shukla, 2000; MacD[illegible] et al., 2007; Matson, Kiely, & Bamburg, 1997; Smith & Van Houten, 1996). Stereotypic behaviors include, but are not limited to, repetitive vocalizations and repetitive body movements (e.g., hand flapping, rocking, tensing, etc.). A very common and challenging behavior to address is vocal stereotypy, sometimes referred to as "scripting." As a parent you may be excited to hear your son or daughter talking, and as a provider these behaviors may be your gateway into teaching new conversational skills. There is a fine line, however, between what is appropriate and useful and that which is inappropriate and interfering with learning. Throughout this chapter, we hope to give you a better understanding of stereotypy in general, and share with you strategies for intervening on the often persistent behavior of vocal stereotypy.

Vocal stereotypy is said to occur when a child says sounds, words, or phrases over and over. This could be random speech, repeating lines or phrases from a television show or movie, repetition of phrases commonly heard in his/her environment, non-contextual laughing, humming, singing songs, shrieks, etc. The form of vocal stereotypy varies across individuals and time. When your child is young, it can be challenging to determine if the child is engaging in problematic stereotypy, as some amount of stereotypy is a part of typical development. When speaking with friends or family, they may reassure you that these behaviors are normal and they have seen their own children engaging in repetitive body movements that may be similar to those of your child, such as hand-flapping when excited. These same friends or family may have also heard their children repeating phrases or even using lines from movies as part of their child's pretend play. The main difference is that as these other children mature, they outgrow these repetitive movements and scripted language, and replace them with appropriate and unscripted play and conversation.

Think back to your childhood. Did someone directly teach you everything you learned? For typically developing children, much of what is learned occurs by observing adults, siblings, or peers, and imitating their actions or speech in the appropriate context with others. Stereotypic behavior can hinder the ability of children with ASD to gain new skills from the general environment (Kennedy et al., 2000; Lovaas, Koegel, Simmons, & Long, 1973). When children with ASD are engaging in stereotypic behaviors, they are not learning from the language that is naturally occurring in their environment. A great deal of language and social interactions are learned from observations such as watching a parent cook in the kitchen or fix a broken chair, or by playing dolls with big sister.

For children who are busy engaging in stereotypy much of the time, lack of attention to such activities could lead to hearing fewer words during a crucial developmental period for language and cognitive abilities. In school, teachers rely on this type of learning in everyday situations. For example, a teacher may plan a lesson for the group using a book about bears. The main goal of the lesson is to introduce students to the idea of sequentially ordering events, but while reading the teacher points out several colors the students have no or minimal exposure to, such as violet. Later, several of the students are observed playing in the block center and trying to decide if some of the blocks are colored violet. If the child is singing, laughing, or repeating a script from TV over and over (i.e., vocal stereotypy) during any of these events, however, then that child has just missed an important opportunity to learn from the everyday situations.

In many classrooms, students are expected to learn through teacher-led instruction, as well as through the observation of peers' actions. If the child is engaged in time-consuming stereotypic behaviors, the child may be unable to learn important social behaviors and academic skills. For instance, in a kindergarten class, a teacher may use a song to teach the class about the order of the days of the week. If the child is engrossed in vocal stereotypy during the song, (s)he may be unable to recall the order of the days of the week when asked at a later time. For older children, it may be a math lesson taught at the beginning of the week that is critical for another lesson to be learned later in the week. If the student is engaged in vocal stereotypy throughout the math lesson, (s)he may be unable to build upon the foundational skills taught at the beginning of the week for the lesson to be taught later in the week.

Another difficulty associated with stereotypic behaviors is that when children are engrossed in these types of behaviors, they are missing time to interact with peers and build peer relationships. The child will have fewer opportunities to have conversations with peers because either the child is too engrossed in stereotypic behavior to take notice that another child would like to talk to them, or the peers will have lost interest in talking to the child because the child is not making sense to them.

Conversation skills become increasingly more important as children move through school and peer relationships become more complex. That is, children move away from game play to more conversational-dependent exchanges. In addition to building peer relationships, social rules and niceties (e.g., saying, 'bless you' when someone sneezes or standing quietly in line), can be more difficult to develop for children with ASD who engage in vocal stereotypy because the child is spending most of her/his time engaging in stereotypic behavior.

As you are most likely aware, many clinicians have tried a variety of treatments to reduce vocal stereotypy. This particular area has proven very challenging due to the behavior typically being very persistent and often maintained by automatic reinforcement. It is important to understand why this behavior is so challenging. In a study that looked at the different functions of stereotypy, 61% of the cases were maintained by only automatic reinforcement (Hanley, Iwata, & McCord, 2003). That is, the reinforcement is the "natural" result of engaging in the behavior. It is thought that engaging in the behavior produces some sort of sensory stimulation and this sensory stimulation functions as a reinforcer. There are various reasons why a child may engage in this behavior, such as the child might like the feeling in their throat when making the sounds/words, they might like hearing themselves talk, or it may be to drown out the noise of other people or the environment around the child (although this last example treads on the line between self-stimulatory and environmental control).

Behavior that is maintained by automatic reinforcement can be very difficult to reduce because no other person is needed to provide reinforcement. Behavioral interventions are most effective when the function of the behavior has been identified, which then allows for a replacement behavior to be taught that will serve the same function as the challenging behavior. For example, a child will scream to get his parent's attention. The function of screaming is to gain parental attention. A replacement behavior would be to teach the child to ask for the parent's attention appropriately, and this would result in gaining the parent's attention. Thus, asking nicely and screaming both serve the same function, getting the parent's attention. With automatic reinforcement, however, no other person is involved in delivering the reinforcer. It can be difficult to find an alternative reinforcer that will directly compete with the current reinforcer (i.e., sensory stimulation: Vollmer, 1994). The challenge with behaviors that are maintained by automatic reinforcement is to find an intervention that focuses on trying to reduce or remove the motivation to engage in the challenging behavior.

One intervention that has been demonstrated to be effective in reducing vocal stereotypy is called Response Interruption and Redirection, or RIRD (Ahearn, Clark, MacDonald, & Chung, 2007; Athens, Vollmer, Sloman, & St. Peter Pipken, 2008; Liu-Gitz & Banda, 2010). This procedure involves prompting a verbal response that is different from the "script" every time the child engages in vocal stereotypy. The premise of this intervention is that by making the child engage in a few demands immediately after vocal stereotypy occurs, it will make engaging in vocal stereotypy a more effortful task. That is, the child has to do a little work every time (s)he engages in vocal stereotypy. Thus, the child will soon learn that every time (s)he makes an inappropriate vocalization, then (s)he will have to do more work.

This type of intervention is typically very effortful for a caregiver to conduct, but the research literature has shown it to be an effective technique. Given that vocal stereotypy can be such a stigmatizing and interfering behavior, it would seem to warrant the effort necessary to conduct this intervention. When beginning this intervention, it should be conducted for short periods of time throughout the day and in an area that minimizes distractions, such as sitting at a table. Carrying out the treatment in such a setting will not only help the child learn to understand the intervention, but it will help the caregiver maintain the ability to implement the intervention accurately. We would suggest conducting the intervention for 5 minutes at a time, with the child in a neutral area that does not feature excessive stimulation or possible alternate activities (to avoid competing for student attention/engagement). It is best that the only focus that caregiver has when starting the intervention is to step in and conduct the intervention, as opposed to attempting to teach the child other skills while conducting the intervention at the same time. As the child becomes familiar with the contingencies in place for vocal stereotypy, adding in additional activities and generalizing locations will be important steps in preparation for successfully implementing this procedure throughout the child's day. In order for the child to understand when you are conducting the intervention compared to when you are not conducting the intervention, use some type of signal for the child. This could be done by using card that is one color (e.g., red) on one side and a different color (e.g., green) on the other side, or putting a watch/bracelet on the child. When this signal is presented to the child, you can say a simple phase such as, "Angela, the watch is on, it is time for good talking" or a similar statement. When the child engages in vocal stereotypy, the caregiver will immediately interrupt the child by saying, "No, Angela," or "Nope, let's try again," and redirect the child to engage in alternate vocalizations (i.e., say something else that will be appropriate to the situation). The caregiver will give the child three consecutive prompts for appropriate vocalizations. The child will need to respond to the prompts and not engage in vocal stereotypy during the set of three prompts, and then the caregiver will provide some praise for engaging in appropriate vocalizations. The vocal prompt can be either imitation of a word (e.g., "Say, 'horse'") or answering simple questions such as, "What is it?" when presenting an object, or "What is your name?" The words or questions that are used during this intervention need to be based on the child's vocal abilities. The child should be able to easily imitate the words or answer the questions that are used during the intervention, as this is not a time for teaching new skills. In fact, if the child answers your question or imitates incorrectly, it should still be considered one of the three responses needed to exit the intervention. If the child cannot imitate words or sounds easily, some research has indicated that the use of prompts for nonverbal behavior such as touching head or clapping hands upon request, are effective in reducing vocal stereotypy (Shepherd, 2010, unpublished master thesis). The prompted motor skills can be any non-vocal imitation skill or receptive direction that is within the child's repertoire. If the child engages in vocal stereotypy during any of the three directions, then the child will be prompted to engage in three more vocal/motor tasks before receiving praise for engaging in the appropriate response. At any time during this intervention, the caregiver should be providing reinforcement for any appropriate vocalizations. For example, if the child makes an appropriate request, please honor it if possible.

An example of using vocal demands might look like this:

Angela engages in vocal stereotypy.

Teacher says, "No. Let's try again. What color?" (showing blue car)

Angela says, "Blue."

Teacher says, "What is your name?"

Angela says, "Angela."

Teacher says, "Say, dog."

Angela says, "Dog."

Teacher says, "Fantastic!"

An example of using motor demands might look like this:

The child engages in vocal stereotypy.

The parent states, "Nope, let's try again. Do this," and the parent touches her own nose.

The child engages in the correct response.

The parent presents the next demand, "Do this" and the parent stomps her feet.

The child imitates the motor response.

The parent presents a third demand, “Clap your hands.”

The child engages in the correct response.

The parent provides a praise statement, “You got it!” in an excited voice.

As soon as the intervention session is over, it is important to signal to the child that the intervention is no longer being conducted. Thus, the caregiver should make it apparent, for example by turning the card over to the other side or taking off the watch/bracelet. This can also be paired with a statement informing the child that the intervention is no longer in place, such as, “It’s free time.” It is very important to use consistent signals for the child, as this will help the child to understand when the intervention is in place and when it is not in place. If these signals are not clear, it could lead to vocal stereotypy resurfacing when it had previously been reduced.

When the caregiver has seen a reduction in the frequency of needing to use the RIRD procedure during the 5 minute intervention sessions, they should then start increasing the duration of the intervention and start running the intervention when the child is learning some other skills.

There are several questions that can arise during the implementation of this intervention. First, if you are unsure if what the child is engaging in is vocal stereotypy, lean towards implementing the intervention. This may require you or the treatment team to adjust your behavioral definition. It is common for the child to engage in new forms of vocal stereotypy during this intervention. For example a child may go from singing a song to softly humming a tune.

Second, when conducting this intervention, it is common for the child to refuse to comply with the vocal/motor direction. This is where the caregiver must be persistent and continue to present the vocal/motor direction, around every 5 seconds, until the child complies. It can be frustrating for the person implementing the intervention, but it is important to maintain the integrity of the intervention. We have found that refusals to engage in the vocal/motor tasks are typically going to take place if your child/client has not previously been in a situation where follow-through on instructions was the norm. Even for these children, the refusals, though frequent and long during that particular session, were short-lived across the sessions. It is also important to decide ahead of time how you will handle any other problem behaviors that arise during the implementation of this procedure. In our experience, it is best to focus solely on vocal stereotypy until it has been reduced before adding in additional consequences for other problem behaviors.

Lastly, once the child has been signaled that the intervention is over, it is typical for the child to engage in a burst of vocal stereotypy or engage in vocal stereotypy when the intervention is not in place. Parents/providers should not be alarmed if this is occurring, as long as the child is not doing the same thing during the intervention. It will be important to collect data so you are able to ascertain when the procedure has become effective and if it remains effective as you generalize the activities occurring during intervention and increase the amount of time running the RIRD procedure.

It should be noted that a complete elimination of vocal stereotypy may not happen for a long time, or ever, even when the intervention is present. The goal of this intervention should be to reduce vocal stereotypy to a level that will allow the child to learn from their environment, by slowly and systematically increasing the amount of the day in which the intervention is in place. This will, in turn, allow you to "turn off" the intervention at times of day that would be appropriate for the child to engage in vocal stereotypy. These could include recess, the car ride home from school, or leisure time after dinner. When we have used this invention with children in an early intervention program and classroom settings, the children were initially resistant to the intervention during the initial sessions, but over time learned to understand the contingency, which then resulted in more time to teach these children important skills such as language and social skills that allowed them to have more of a role in family activities.

"This morning, like the past few mornings, have been miracle days," Beatrice thinks to herself as she drives Jordana to school. Not only did they get up, get dressed, and were out

the door on time, but Beatrice did not have to continually ask Jordana to get her shoes, bag, jacket, etc. The lines from the Jordana's beloved TV shows and movies were barely uttered during the entire morning. It has been a few weeks since the consultant started working with Jordana to reduce her scripting and Beatrice is amazed with her daughter's progress and how much this has positively affected the family as whole.

"Hi, Jordana! How are you today?" Mr. Larkins is very proud of how far Jordana has come in just the few short weeks since the consultant started the new procedure for the once persistent vocal stereotypy. "I'm good, how are you?" Jordana replies. Rarely would she have answered a question without multiple prompts to pause her scripting and reply. Mr. Larkins sees many new opportunities opening up for Jordana's future.

Chapter Five

Clothing: What Ever Shall I Wear?

Alexandra Brown

Clothes. Let's face it, we all gotta wear them. They can be long, short, smooth, rough, loose, tight, you name it. They change depending on the weather, season, or where you're going. If you have autism, understanding the "clothing rules of the world" can be impossible, or clothes could be a source of inflexible behavior.

Let's consider Sienna, a four year old girl with blonde curls, cute as a button. If Sienna wore clothing that had a zipper on it, the zip had to be done right up to the top, every time, no exceptions. Big deal? Let it go? She's so cute, what does it matter? If we took this attitude, however, experience has shown us that this beautiful little girl would only eat from a pink plate, with a specific mat under it, only in pink clothes, while wearing a tiara. The "zip up to the top" was the latest in a long line of inflexibilities, fortunately each one becoming easier to crack as we continued our work.

The process used with Sienna, from her team of fabulous therapists and supportive parents, was systematic desensitization. The general steps of a systematic desensitization plan include:

1. Teach a calming/coping skill.
2. Create a hierarchy from least troubling to most troubling stimuli.
3. Gradually exposing the student to that which is troubling, slowly and systematically, minimizing upset.

Sienna was first taught some calming techniques to help her to self-manage when she became upset. Sienna would then receive reinforcement for leaving the zipper in a specific up/down/in the middle position for the time specified at the current level of the procedure. Moving onto the next level was dependent upon zero occurrences of crying, attempting to move the zipper, or vocalizations such as "it's too tight" (which didn't really make sense given the position). To give an idea of our hierarchy of positions, step one was lowering the zipper, whilst on, for one second. The final step was ensuring that Sienna could wear a variety of zipped tops, and wear the zip at any position. Gradually, the screams became a whine. The whine became a stern "I don't like it." "I don't like it" became a terse "OK." Eventually, there was no noticeable response at all. Sienna may never love having her zip at different levels, but she accepts it without fussing. An example of the application of this procedure occurred just the other day. Sienna has just started to ride in a car without a car seat. Due to her new difference in height, the seat belt is at a slightly higher level and could catch the edge of her face. Sienna made attempts to adjust the seat belt, to no avail. I looked at her jacket. It had a zip. I took a deep breath, and said "what about this?" as I unzipped the jacket half way and wrapped it around the seatbelt as a makeshift protector. "OK," said Sienna, sounding calm as can be.

I'll be honest, it's not always that easy with every child. Sienna has acquired a great deal of language and is starting to understand many of life's social rules. It also helps that she has received 30-40 hours of therapy a week for the past two and a half years. This wasn't the first thing we jumped into, ensuring that Sienna had some understanding of what we were doing.

Taking another example, let's consider Ben. Ben has just turned two and loves his clothes. Yes, this kid *really* loves his clothes. Bath time is a nightmare, the most dreaded part of the day for all involved. The removal of Ben's clothing is a battle. He will cry, scream, point to them, and reach for them. His behavior would indicate that all he wants of the world are those clothes on his back. He can work himself into a hot little frenzy.

The same passion applies with shoes and socks. There's an unwritten rule governing when they come off and when they go on. Each time is like a re-enactment of the Battle of Waterloo. Ben is in the early stages of therapy. He has learned, "to get X, I do Y." Good start. In a few short weeks, his response to showers has been steadily improving. He will take off his own shoes, if the context is blaringly obvious, but his therapist has to takes hers off too. We're working on getting rid of that requirement: baby steps!

These odd little clothes inflexibilities start off small. You can get through your day by letting them go. But, make no mistake, they grow. They grow so much that your entire day can revolve around them. They can take over your life. What do you do when the only yellow shirt that Sam will wear is in the washing machine? It's time to leave the house and he's screaming for it. It was cute when he was three, but now at five, it's not quite as cute. He's bigger and stronger and has had lots of time to practice being inflexible. It's nearly time to start school and the idea of getting him into a uniform is unfathomable. Not to mention the fact that the shirt is getting too small and holey, and washing it needs to be carefully planned.

The clothing issue can also quickly spread to other forms. Think about costumes. In the world of autism spectrum disorders, this often takes the form of superhero outfits. I remember one particular therapy session with a very cross four year old, whose Teenage Mutant Ninja Turtles costume was drying on the line. He was sitting there in his underpants. We used the almost-dry costume as a reinforcer for putting on a sock for just one second. It built from there. Luckily, or actually through a ton of hard work by parents and team rather than luck, now at ten years of age, this boy wouldn't be caught dead admitting to his TMNT infatuation. He wears civilian clothes now!

So, you've done the hard yards to ensure that your child will wear a variety of clothes, will take those clothes off when asked, and will wear them in different ways. Suddenly, summer hits! Out go the long sleeves and pants, in come the t-shirts and shorts. "Hooray," we all say! Many children on the spectrum, however, shriek "Whaaaat!?!?!" Others, like Ben, look distraught, frantically pulling at their short sleeves to see if the next tug will be the lucky one that extends those short sleeves to their wrists. For the children who can understand, we must prepare them: "The next term, the uniform changes. You'll pack those clothes away until next year and wear the dress until fall." For the children who don't yet have the language, show them. Keep your language simple: "Look, short, hot." They may still pull their sleeves down frantically at first, but daily practice will ensure that this fades away.

Hamish, a very bright four year old, used to share the clothing obsession with Ben. When the first warm weather of spring hit, Hamish was put in short sleeves by his mother. In the past it would be a tantrum. Nowadays it's an acknowledging comment: "I wear short sleeves in spring." It just so happened to be the first day of spring, and we couldn't help but feel that this may have helped Hamish make sense of it, and perhaps tolerate it better that day.

"Because he has autism." That's not a reason, that's an excuse. There is no excuse for a child to wear a knitted sweater when its 100 degrees outside, leading to possible heat stroke, or carrying a child wearing only underwear and wrapped in a blanket to a car waiting outside during a blizzard. Behavior can be changed. Behavior changes slowly and gradually, sometimes, and there may be some tantrums along the way. But it's all worth it in the end, to look at your child and see how far he or she has come. It's worth all the hard work to ensure that the yellow shirt doesn't take over someone's life. ABA gives us the tools to do this in the most efficient and fun way for all concerned. Learn it, live it and you'll come to love it.

Chapter Six

The Importance of Teaching Daily Living Skills

Lisa M. Swift

In this chapter, I will discuss the challenges of teaching self help skills to adolescent students diagnosed with autism spectrum disorders. Activities of daily living (ADLs) are vital skills to teach children diagnosed with autism spectrum disorders (ASD). Teaching these skills in every day situations is often overlooked, however. There is an understandable emphasis on teaching language and academic skills, and a child's day is often scheduled to include multiple therapy sessions and social skills groups. ADLs can get lost in there. While the other skills mentioned are of course very important, some of the most valuable skills to teach can be done on a routine basis throughout the day. No special therapy is required.

Teaching ADL skills like dressing, grooming, and appropriate eating provides independence and social acceptance in society. They are the very tools that are needed to function in a less restrictive environment, secure a job, and enjoy a better quality of life. There are also many challenges that arise which hinder the ability of children diagnosed with ASD to acquire these skills easily. As a result, it generally requires more teaching time, and often more systematic efforts.

Teaching daily living skills can be very challenging. Children diagnosed on the autism spectrum need to be explicitly taught how to perform these skills and it is often hard for them to imitate what their caregiver or teacher is showing them without specific training. Also, many children with ASD may have weak fine and gross motor skills. Getting dressed and manipulating clothing with buttons, zippers, and snaps is difficult. There can also be a sensory component in which the child is tactile defensive towards taste or texture. Additionally, social awareness plays a role. A child with ASD may not be motivated to bathe or brush their teeth the same way a typically developing child would, because they do not understand the social implications that can arise. Finally, caregivers and teachers may avoid teaching these skills because the student engages in problem behavior during these teaching times (remember, it is difficult for the student to acquire these skills and thus there may be resistance to practice!). All these challenges make it exhausting to "battle it out" on an everyday basis. As difficult as it may be, look down the road 10, 15, 20 years. It is only going to get worse when the child is older, as was the case with Lucy.

Lucy was a 17 year old young lady diagnosed with moderate autism, who attended a local special education school. Lucy's mother was trying to prepare for Lucy's transition from high school to adult services and visited a day rehabilitation program in the community. Lucy's mother really liked the program. One of the requirements for her daughter's acceptance, however, was independent toileting skills.

Lucy's mother was panicking because her daughter always needed physical assistance in the bathroom. In fact, Lucy was never taught to use toilet paper, wipe effectively, or to wash her hands without help. Lucy's mother explained that it became routine to just help Lucy when she went to the bathroom. Now, Lucy's mother was desperate to teach her daughter these skills, as it was going to greatly impact her acceptance into adult programs.

A treatment package was created that included:

1. A task analysis of skills
2. A backward chaining procedure
3. Training sessions to teach the mother how to teach each skill and fade prompts.

The general strategy of a task analysis is that one creates a detailed list of every step that must be completed to complete a long behavior chain (like washing one's hands). A backward chaining procedure is one in which the student is taught the last step in the chain first. Once (s)he is performing that skill, we work on the last step AND the next to last step, working backwards in our list. To take an example from the world of dressing, teaching putting on a shirt via a backward chain would entail putting the shirt on the student and teaching tucking in as a last step. Once this is mastered, one would put the shirt on the student, but they would learn to pull it down and tuck it in, etc.

As Lucy mastered each step in her task analysis, the next step was taught until she had mastered the entire skill set. Initially, Lucy was resistant and started to engage in problem behavior when requested to complete a task. I explained that this was normal. She had never had to perform these skills before and now was being asked to do so after 17 years. Lucy's mother carried out the plan, and after several days, noticed Lucy was complying with more requests. Within a few weeks, Lucy could care for her bathroom needs with vocal prompting. After a month of implementing the treatment plan every day, Lucy was independent with using the bathroom.

There are many stories like Lucy's, and it often takes crisis events such as the requirements of the new program to start working on skills to promote independence. Lucy's mother was thrilled with the progress her daughter made and looked forward to her future. Lucy's mother was also excited because day-to-day life became easier for Lucy, as well as the rest of the family.

When a child diagnosed with ASD is toilet trained, we often focus only on the child voiding in the toilet. Sometimes caregivers and teachers get into the habit of wiping the child's bottom after he uses the toilet, pull up his pants, and help him to wash his hands after going to the bathroom. Let's face it, it saves time and it's much easier than the alternative. Unfortunately, we are inadvertently disabling the child further. The child needs to be taught to manage his own clothing, wipe after urinating or having a bowl movement, and wash his hands. All these skills need to be learned in order to successfully master using the bathroom independently. Several tactics described in the literature can be used to teach dressing and hand washing skills. As alluded to above, according to Cooper, Heron, and Heward (1987), backward chaining is the process by which behaviors are learned when the child completes all the steps in a behavior chain except the last step. As each training step is mastered, reinforcement is delivered. After the last step is mastered the second to last step is targeted and so on until the student can complete all the steps in the sequence successfully.

Grooming (e.g., brushing teeth and combing hair) skills are imperative to teach, but are often difficult to address under daily time constraints. The child may help brush his teeth, your hand over his hand, but continuing to do this over the years can lead to prompt dependence if the hand over hand prompt is not faded. Brushing one's teeth is a complex skill. When task analyzed, however, it can be taught in smaller, more manageable steps. Again as described above, a task analysis is defined by Cooper, et al. (1987) as "a procedure in which complex behaviors are broken down into smaller components." Horner and Keilitz (1975) developed a tooth brushing program that included a task analysis and teaching procedure. In their study, all eight participants showed improvement in each component of the task using the very straight-forward task analysis and teaching procedure as described above.

Showering is another difficult task that caregivers of children diagnosed with ASD may have to address. There are times when children are "scared" of taking a shower/bath. Often, the caregiver may not bathe the child every day because it is a struggle. When they do bathe the child, they may wash him/her as quickly as possible to avoid or reduce the child's tendency to engage in problem behavior. Unfortunately, tiptoeing around this crucial skill will make it much more difficult to tackle later on as the child gets older, stronger, and bigger (not to mention, there are also social implications). It's not difficult to help your child bathe when he is 5 years old. It gets complicated, however, when he is 25 years old. The Premack Principle, or pairing procedure, can be used to help decrease problem behavior. The Premack Principle (Premack, 1959) requires a child to perform a less desired activity before he has access to a highly desired activity. Making it practical, after the child takes a bath he can watch his favorite television show or play with his favorite toy if he does not engage in problem behavior (watching the show or playing with the toy being more highly desired by the child than bathing). If the child does not engage in the less desired behavior (bathing) or engages in problem behavior, then he does not get his reinforcer (television or favorite toy). When this procedure is used, the child does not have access to the reward at any other time of the day to keep motivation high. You can also attempt to cushion the effort by the use of a pairing procedure. A pairing procedure is used to increase the value of a less desirable activity (bath time) by associating this activity with a highly preferred activity (e.g., reading the child's favorite book while he is bathing).

You may undertake this effort in stages. Start with a small interval of time and slowly increase the time the child is in the bath as he becomes more comfortable. Once the child takes a bath or shower without any behavioral issues, you can use a task analysis or chaining procedure to teach the child proper washing skills.

Another important set of skills that are not always explicitly taught are preparing meals and eating. Many times, simple meals are prepared for kids and all they need to do is show up to eat. Ketchup is already squeezed out of the bottle and is ready for french fries to be dipped; the child's drink is opened and poured into a cup of ice, the meal is cut into small manageable pieces so the child does not have to use a knife. This is a fine arrangement for a toddler, but as the child gets older he will need to learn to do these skills for himself.

Humans are highly motivated by eating, especially their favorite foods. As a caregiver or teacher, you can use this to your advantage and teach the child to open containers or bags, eat using utensils, and even prepare simple meals. Johnson and Cuvo (1981) used pictorial recipes to teach adults with developmental disabilities how to cook, and Thinesen and Bryan (1981) taught individuals with developmental disabilities meal preparation. Picture schedules and visual cues can help promote independence and teach children diagnosed with ASD to complete steps in complex tasks.

Teaching daily living and self-help skills to children diagnosed with ASD is just as important as teaching language skills and academic skills. The lives of children with ASD and their families can drastically change and their futures become more fulfilling. Setting up time during the day and dealing with the challenges that unfold will not matter in your memory when your child, now an adult, is successful and independent in these basic areas.

Chapter Seven

Going out to Eat

Alison Roberts

There are so many stories to tell regarding this topic, but one in particular comes to mind immediately. There is a family that I have been working with for several years. Each year, they get together with their entire family for holidays and go out to eat. A few years ago, it was brought to my attention that the child in this family was starting to have difficulty during these events. One specific occasion that brought everything to a head and caused the family to go into a panic and seek help, was when they told me about their Christmas dinner.

The Johnsons went out for Christmas dinner to a very nice restaurant, where they were meeting all of Mrs. Johnson's family. Before entering the restaurant, their daughter Michelle started to verbally protest about going into the restaurant. Mom reminded her that after they ate they could go to the gift shop and purchase an item. Each year, Michelle was allowed to purchase a new stuffed animal from the gift shop of this familiar restaurant. Michelle sat down with everyone, but as the family was ordering their appetizers she began to whine. Mom assured Michelle that she would be getting her french fries soon. The whine turned into a yell and at this point dad was getting very upset, watching people look at his daughter. Mom kept talking to Michelle and trying to calm her down. Dad, in a firm voice, told her to "STOP," which then turned Michelle's yelling into to a full blood-curdling scream. Dad immediately stood up and told Michelle to go to the car with him. Dad thought it was best to remove himself and Michelle from the restaurant before he would get into an altercation with someone who might say something hurtful towards his child. "The looks" were glaring right at his disabled daughter. While everyone else finished their dinner, dad sat in his car with Michelle screaming about how she wanted to go home. Dad was able to work through this challenge in the car (by screaming at her) but desperately wanted and needed the tools to be able to go out with his child again and feel comfortable doing so.

For some of you, going out to eat is an everyday event, while others look forward to one day going out as a family to eat. Unfortunately, there are also those who can't even imagine such a family event ever happening. Hopefully, by the end of this chapter, you will all feel differently and be ready to take the next step.

Before going into procedures that may be used to help complete this task with success, I would like to provide you with a task analysis for going out to eat, with behaviors that will be "filled in" for each step:

1. Leaving the house
2. Walking to the car
3. Going in the car
4. Driving to the restaurant

5. Getting out of the car
6. Walking to the restaurant
7. Walking in the restaurant
8. Asking for a table
9. May have to wait for table
10. Sitting at table
11. Looking at menu
12. Ordering
13. Wait, Wait, Wait, Wait, Wait
14. Receiving food
15. Eating
16. May wait if dessert is ordered
17. Wait, Wait, Wait, Wait, Wait
18. Receiving check
19. Paying
20. Walking to door
21. Leaving restaurant
22. Walking to car
23. Going in car
24. Driving home

Although this list can be very intimidating, it is necessary to go through it and see where your child has difficulty and start at the previous step. For example, if your child can walk into the restaurant but has difficulty waiting for his/her food, then find a place where you can order your child's food in advance. Gradually, increase the time waiting for food. It would also help move things along if we work on waiting in all environments where the behavior must be displayed (home, school, community, etc.). It seems odd to say, but in this day and age, our children may actually stand out if they *do not* have some hand-held device with them. Bring your devices and use them to reinforce appropriate behavior and waiting.

If your child has a very limited food repertoire, but can sit and wait in a restaurant, then call ahead and tell the restaurant that your child has allergies. You may be able to bring his/her food from home or order a small item that may not be eaten by the child. At home, continue to work on increasing the repertoire and purchase items from restaurants, and introduce the foods at home.

For those children who need to know when the food is coming, set up an activity schedule for going out to eat. For those of you who are unfamiliar with activity schedules, it is suggested to pick up Krantz and McClannahan's, *Activity Schedules for Children with Autism Teaching Independent Behavior, 2nd Edition.* It is a very easy read and it will help assist in setting up a schedule. Remember to reinforce appropriate use of the schedule!

An additional piece of advice is to seek out specific factors that might make things easier for your child. For those of you who have heard that your child does great going out to eat with his/her class during the school day, for example, then:

1. Ask what specific procedures, if any, are used.
2. Have them describe the child's behavior.
3. If possible, observe your child or ask if they could be videotaped in that environment.

For those of you that receive ABA hours at home, rather than having the session in the house, go into the community. When you begin this process, take along people who will provide positive support. This task could be challenging, and you may need to have the hands to ensure that everyone meets success.

Thanks to some amazing moms (Melissa, Jeanne, and Mary) here are a few more tips that may help you.

1. If your child can tolerate noise, go to the restaurant with some noise, so if your child is having a difficult time, it will be less noticeable.
2. The first few times you go out, go during off hours (early, before the crowds, not on Friday or Saturday night). Gradually introduce larger and larger crowds.
3. ALWAYS make a reservation.
4. Go online and check for the restaurant's website. View and print the menu and ask everyone who is going out to dinner to make their selection before you go. It will save time initially.
5. If you are planning on ordering appetizers/desserts and your child may not like what the restaurant has to offer, bring your own food (if allowed) or activity for that time.
6. If a schedule is not used, an alternative that may work is a timer. Set the timer for a longer interval than you plan on staying and let your child know that you will leave when the timer goes off. Of course you can leave early but it will be on your terms. Just make sure you keep an eye on the timer to make sure it doesn't go off before you are finished. Be prepared to make the first visits very short. In some cases, you may not eat at all, but simply visit the restaurant and leave before ordering as an early step in the task analysis.
7. For those of you who don't like to plan your entire day or who are married to someone who doesn't, place a bag in the car with everything you may need when you go out to eat. This way you will always be ready.
8. The more you go, the more comfortable you will be.

This skill set may take weeks or months to master, but when your child acquires it, (s)he will have it for the rest of his/her life. So, rather than staying home for the holidays or parties or getting a babysitter, empower your child with this skill that will help him/her, as well as your entire family.

Chapter Eight

You Are What You Reap, And You Eat What You Sow

Stella Spanakos and Patrick Bardsley

Stella

Ollie: *"Well, here's another nice mess you've gotten me into."*

This story is about my son Nicholas, who is 19 years old, severely autistic, has no expressive language and uses a litewriter to communicate.

How did you get me into this mess Stanley*?*

Oh, I remember: life, a husband, trying to have some sort of semblance of a "normal" life, trying to hold it all together as a wife, mother, and not take this all too seriously or someone would surely find me dead on the kitchen floor from an overdose of Ben and Jerry's Cherry Garcia Frozen Yogurt.

It's not like I didn't know better! I taught for fifteen years before my son was born. I retired from teaching to re-educate myself in a field of education I knew very little about, autism. I wanted to work with my son and his team of therapists and teachers full time because I couldn't believe how ignorant I was about autism and ABA.

Nicholas was so tactilely defensive, when I tried to introduce baby cereal, he promptly responded by projectile vomiting all over Mommy! Mind you, I am the eldest of five. I grew up with a sibling attached to my hip until I left for college. I have fed a lot of babies in my lifetime and that was a first for me! I was entering the abyss; it was the beginning of . . . . "food nightmare."

I had to puree the strained baby food in order for it to be texture-free so that Mommy wouldn't have to wear it! (Although, I had gotten rather good at protective gear, I looked something like a welder feeding a baby!) It took us years. I say *us* because Nicholas' speech therapist, Susan Gilbert, started working with him from age 2.5 until she retired in 2009.

It took us three years before Nicholas would eat "junior" foods without sharing them with us! Our favorite joke was, a sense of humor is mandatory when dealing with autistic offspring; and there could be worse things in life than serving pureed foods at Nicholas' wedding. If nothing else, the senior guests would love it!

Nicholas was six when he entered kindergarten; by then he was able to tolerate a soft sandwich. By soft, I mean creamy peanut butter, fruit spreads with no seeds on white bread, no crust, which mommy had to cut up into triangles, not squares, but triangles because he was obsessed with Sesame Street's Telly Monster and the Secret Triangle Lovers Club video. Ah, the things we do for love and survival.

My immediate goal in life was to find things my son would eat. I used to worry sick about how I was going to meet his nutritional needs when he abruptly stopped drinking milk. No juice, just water in his bottle and that was another part of the problem; Nicholas had such poor oral motor skills that transitioning to a cup was just the icing on my cake!

As time passed, I was so grateful that I could get Nicholas to eat anything at all, that we got into this ritual where I would literally sit and play with him in his room using whatever it took: videos, CDs, computer games. I had no pride, I was so desperate and thrilled to see him eat that it didn't matter where or what so long as he ate. Yes, it felt like I was living Dr. Seuss' "Green Eggs and Ham" book every day of my adult life!

Nicholas, would you could you in your room?

Would you could you for a balloon?

Could you eat this here or there?

But please, dear Nicholas just eat this anywhere!

And so dear reader can you see, how this situation began

Consuming me?

Eventually, through our painstaking efforts, Nicholas started eating a variety of foods and textures. Even presently, at age nineteen, there are many things Nicholas won't eat; he is still a work in progress. In other words, all the guests at his wedding will now be eating chicken fingers and fries!

My husband, Paul, did not get home from work until late, and he loved the Greek tradition of eating dinner late and going to sleep on a full stomach. This led me to the habit of letting Nicholas eat wherever he wanted to (usually his play room, which was off my kitchen) so I could cook dinner and watch him. I spent my days fighting battles and wars with my son. He displayed life-threatening behaviors (like running towards cars in the street), no expressive language, and a communication disorder. Do you know what it's like to run around a house frantically screaming: "Nicholas where are you?" and hearing dead silence because your child just doesn't get it? I am a woman who played men's ice hockey; I have no fear, but this use to bring me to my knees with panic attacks! I was so desperate for this child's safety that I actually asked my vet if it were possible to put a chip in my son for tracking purposes! I was so exhausted by the end of the day that I just didn't have another fight in me when it came to the "let's eat at the table" part of the curriculum. I was consciously ignoring the problem, or monster, I had created.

In 2006, my son was assigned a new 1:1 counselor at camp, and so began a very special relationship between an eighteen-year-old British student, a fourteen-year-old boy with autism, and his family. I knew Patrick was special from the first e-mail he sent me. He knew things about my son that only I knew; not even his father knew Nicholas like that. During his undergraduate years in England, I asked Patrick to consider going to graduate school in New York, do the course work for a BCBA and stay in the field of autism because he had more raw talent and ability than many BCBAs I've worked with. So it came to pass that Patrick matriculated at a local university here in New York for his Masters Degree in Special Education and started his life as an "Englishman in New York" (his theme song by Sting).

The relationship that has developed between Patrick and Nicholas, now twenty-three and nineteen, respectively, has just been a pleasure to watch and has filled many voids for me as a parent that I will never experience because Nicholas is an only child.

Even my husband liked Patrick, and that is amazing because my husband liked no one! Patrick helped him understand what it was like to be Nicholas. In some crazy way, he reached my husband where I could not. This has been one of the most comforting thoughts I have had during this past year.

On the evening of June 7th, 2010, my daily schedule and life as I knew it came to an abrupt end. I came home at 10:45 p.m. from a business meeting to find two unmarked police cars, three NYC detectives, and Patrick waiting for me in the driveway. One of them held a picture of Paul; I knew it could only mean one thing. Paul was dead. They informed me that my husband had a massive heart attack and died that evening in flight to Vegas (he was a professional poker player going to compete at the World Series of Poker).

I made the decision to send Patrick and Nicholas up to camp early for many reasons, the most important of which was that I could not have them see me in such a state! Because, let's be real, it is the mothers of the world that are the cement which bond families, make the holidays happen, kiss all wounds and promise to have cookies made for school tomorrow, in addition to our day jobs. I was a wreck and needed the summer months to get ready for their return, develop a new schedule for the school year, and figure out what I was going to do with the rest of my life.

When Patrick and Nicholas returned home from camp, I changed the furniture in the family room (because neither Patrick nor I would sit in Paul's chair), gave Nicholas his own bedroom, and told Patrick, "Welcome to the new beginning." By that, I meant now that it was just the three of us, it was time to address "dinner at the table" with Patrick and Mommy!

Truthfully, Nicholas has really matured so much this past year that I was shocked by his reaction. Just visualize a 5'10", 185 pound male with a five o'clock shadow jump out of his chair and throw himself on your kitchen floor in a full blown tantrum, while the family pets are running for shelter. (And now you know why cocktails are served before dinner!) Well, Mommy was not expecting this reaction. This was just what the doctor ordered: another helping of stress topped with an ulcer and insomnia, but I created the "Food Monster" and now I needed to address it (with Patrick's help, of course)!

What happened to cause such a violent reaction to an invitation to dine with Mommy and Patrick? After several repeat performances of Nicholas throwing tantrums with the family pets looking for shelter at dinnertime, and much discussion, we agreed on a plan of action.

I must say it has been very therapeutic to tell this story, but it is now time to let Patrick weigh in with his perspective. Patrick's following analogy is very interesting and spot on as to how Nicholas views food and the art of eating. I told you the manchild was smart!

Patrick

It would be fair to say that very few people get much pleasure at all from putting gas in their vehicle. And why would they? With rising fuel costs, concerns about carbon emissions, and what we are *personally* doing to the environment, it's little wonder anyone who doesn't have shares in 'Shell' or 'BP' would enjoy it. But that's not really the point; the truth is that putting fuel in your vehicle is almost always part of your day or week that passes you by with little reflection. It's a chore, something we *have* to do, but seldom something we either treasure or ponder.

So imagine the following scenario, if you will. It's Monday morning and you absent-mindedly pull up to "the pump." Allowing your well-established schema for this process to take over, you begin blasting fuel into your vehicle for the next 3 minutes or so (time will vary depending on tank size, outside temperature, and recent foreign policy). On this particular occasion, however, someone is directly forcing you to elongate this process. Suddenly, you are faced with a series of logic-defying demands such as "pump slowly," or "quiet pumping," or my personal favorite, "5 pumps, then take a break." Furthermore, throughout this bemusing ordeal you are being reminded to "stand nicely," to "keep a quiet mouth and hands," and to generally adhere to all the "fuel time" etiquette rules someone has sprung on you.

I trust by now you have recognized the analogy to meal times in our house. I truly believe Nicholas sees no logic in ever "spanning out" a meal. For him, eating is exactly that, a fueling process. It is something he needs to do about 3 times daily, but not necessarily an event he either loves or loathes. So, you can imagine his utter disdain and very apparent frustration (he didn't hide it well), when it was passed into law that all future meals were to take place at the kitchen table, for a minimum of 10 minutes, with a regime of strict and proper meal time decorum. Along with Nicholas' mother Stella, (who could teach Emily Post a thing or two about etiquette!) I felt confident we would emerge victorious and relatively unscathed. To paraphrase Homer Simpson: "*The war was over and the future won, the past never had a chance, man.*" Or as we so fantastically naively thought . . .

Meal times during the ensuing weeks rivaled the intensity of protest that sparked the revolution and subsequent overthrowing of the incumbent government in Egypt at the start of 2011. Nicholas was digging deep into his dusty bag of remonstration behaviors, ("dusty," as many of these behaviors had rarely been seen in years) and meal times immediately transformed into a series of epic battles to get him to sit down, to eat at the table, to stay within a 1-mile radius beyond the period of food consumption!

Needless to say, the war was certainly not over, and I personally was considering emulating former President Mubarak and handing in my notice any day. Then came the meal of absolute enlightenment. Truthfully, things had began to improve prior to this day, for instance he was sitting down at the table during meal times- I shan't say willingly, but he seemed to recognize this new regulation. Also, (with varied levels of prompting) he was beginning to ingest his food at a more typical land mammal pace. Getting him to remain at the table, however, for any length of period following eating still seemed so foreign and frankly downright unreasonable to him.

But, if he had accepted sitting at the table and eating his food in a more appropriate manner, what was so excruciating about sitting there for another 5 minutes afterwards? Following a somewhat informal functional analysis, we decided that although it may well be our company, the strongest contributing factor to his unrest was the uncertainty regarding the whole task completion time. Perhaps making the expected time of the whole task visible in the form of a timer would help? *I can almost hear the 'Duhs'*

It seems so elementary in retrospect. One of the unavoidable consequences of caring about anything is that our ability to think logically and objectively can be jeopardized and we often get caught "looking at the puzzle through a key hole." In this instance, we were so overjoyed that he was voluntarily sitting at the table to eat that we couldn't comprehend the obvious turmoil he was experiencing in sitting there for an unspecified time once he'd finished eating- once he felt the task was over. All this time we were attempting to achieve different tasks, and I hold my emotions (along with the back-patting) fully and inexplicably accountable. Once the timer was set, he sat content for the whole time and "enjoyed" his meal, while inside I'm certain he was tutting, lightly shaking his head, and sighing, "bloody morons."

An interesting upshot of using the timer that we didn't foresee was that Nicholas' eating speed slowed without any extra prompting or redirection from us. Being the logical individual that he is, he saw that he was going to be sat there for that time no matter what, "so why not spend more time eating and less time watching the timer twiddling my thumbs?" he seemed to muse. Thus, he taught himself a valuable lesson in time management and added to his repertoire of rational skills. Although utterly inadvertent, providing the opportunity for Nicholas to self-teach such a valuable skill was a tremendous achievement. Of course, this time we were careful not to indulge ourselves in goal-shrouding merriment!

So perhaps the war is over and the future did emerge victorious? At the time of writing, the issue of fading the timer is being addressed during every meal at the sleep-away summer camp Nicholas attends for 7 weeks annually. While there, he eats full meals three times daily, at a table of up to 10 people, with the food being served "family style" to promote communication and social interaction. The scene resembles a Norman Rockwell painting and couldn't be more authentic for working on such skills. Traditionally, it must be said, timer fading has been a somewhat non-issue for Nicholas and all reports from camp seem to fall in line with custom, which is wonderful to hear. We'll still approach his return to our kitchen table with a hint of trepidation as the settings are so different, but I'm confident he'll quickly re-adjust.

For his mother, Stella, I can see it means so much to have her son eating around a table with her. As a 23-year-old male with no children of my own, I wouldn't say we share the same maternal instincts, but it's easy to empathize how fundamental this aspect of being a mother is to Stella. She knows her son will probably never readily sit for hours, enjoying a large meal with good company and conversation. He may never see the sense in that. But that's ok. Every time I go to get gas I think of him and the analogy we began with, and by no means will I ever see sense in that.

Chapter Nine

Sleeping in My Own Bed

Gail Quinn

The dawn breaks, birds twitter, and you wake to meet the new day. As your eyes flutter open, you're aware of the crick in your neck, the sensation of your feet hanging over the side of the bed and a core body temperature of 104 degrees. What happened? Oh that's right. The kids are in your bed again. The day is just beginning and you're already exhausted from another night of sleep deprivation. Will this cycle never end?

Sleep struggles are all too common among families with and without children diagnosed with ASD. There are estimates as high as 70% for "co-sleeping" (children sleeping in their parent's room) among families in the United States (Piazza & Fisher, 1991). Cultural conventions determine if this is necessarily viewed as a problem or not.

Regardless of cultural differences, however, if co-sleeping is a product of a child's sleep issues, then it can be a stress-producing condition. Many parents struggle to manage life's daily responsibilities operating under significant sleep deprivation. Research shows that, left untreated, children's sleep issues can persist over years, as behavior is reinforced and habits become fixed (Piazza & Fisher, 1991). If you've planned a "family bed" and you are happy with that arrangement, feel free to skip this chapter. If you have lost and want to reclaim sleep, peace, and privacy, however, then read on. The question that requires an answer is, "How do I get my kid to stay in their own bed?"

There are many approaches out there, but few are supported by empirical evidence (though anecdotal success is reported). Several methods will be discussed here and perhaps one of them makes sense for you and your family.

The first step in a successful sleep problem intervention is the establishment of a clear bedtime routine. A bedtime routine is a ritual that signals to the child that sleep time is imminent. Regular engagement in this sequence of events serves as a reminder of what is expected and becomes a way for the child to wind down. If you don't already have a bedtime routine, create one with the aim of fostering relaxation for your child.

This routine can be as short or as long as you like and should make sense to your family and your child (e.g., bath, brush teeth, final trip to the toilet, glass of water by the bed, read a book, kisses and hugs, lights out, tuck in and parent leaves). Engaging in your child's favorite game of wrestling may not be the best activity to include in a bedtime routine, as remember we're trying to wind down and not rile up. Of course, if wrestling puts your child into a docile trance then go for it. It's all individual to the child.

Regardless of what the routine looks like, it's important that it be consistently practiced night after night. I recommend creating and practicing a bedtime routine for a couple of weeks so it is well-established.

Now that the bedtime routine is taken care of, we can look at potential interventions. Be aware that all of these procedures will affect behavior immediately. Initially, however, behavior change might not be in the direction you want it to go. That is, in all probability things might get worse before they get better.

The reason for this is what we call an extinction burst. This is a *temporary* increase in the magnitude, duration, and/or frequency of behavior. This happens because we are changing the rules of the game and the child will want to find out where the new boundaries are. Therefore, they will *try harder* to get the result that they are accustomed to achieving. For example, if your child comes into your room 3 times in the night before you finally give in and let them stay in your bed, they will likely come into your room 10 times to find out when you are going to finally say "yes" the way you always have in the past. They don't yet know that the new rules mean that you will *never* say yes. Before you begin any intervention, just know that this is likely to occur and gird your loins so you can be ready to stand strong through it. Remember that it's temporary. If you give into an extinction burst, you are making your life incrementally more difficult as you will have to work harder for longer to change behavior after that.

Now we can discuss some interventions. A procedure commonly implemented, and one that you may recognize from the television series "Super Nanny," is that of Planned Ignoring. Once the bedtime routine is complete and lights are out, the first time the child leaves the bed parents give a short, succinct explanation such as, "It's bedtime, back to bed," as they lead the child back to bed with no further discussion, eye contact or cuddles. Each subsequent "out of bed" behavior is treated similarly, except this time there is no vocal explanation given. The parent is not ignoring the child; rather the parent is ignoring the crying, vocal protests, physical protests, and negotiations.

Some parents don't like the idea of ignoring what they perceive as their child's needs. They don't like the idea of the time it will take to work through the likely extinction burst. If you choose this method, establish a baseline frequency of "out of bed" behavior before you begin. This will enable you to measure whether or not this particular intervention is working. If it is working, you should see a decrease in "out of bed" behavior over time.

If a child is able to understand a delayed reinforcement contract, it is advisable to establish one prior to commencing. Choose a reinforcer that will only be accessed for this intervention (i.e., in this case, staying in bed). It might be something the child has wanted for a long time, or it might be his favorite train set. Be mindful to choose something you are willing to live without for a period of time as the "staying in bed" behavior is shaped over time.

Create a contract that includes "rules" and clearly spells out the contingency for accessing the reinforcer. The contract might read something like: "If you leave bed fewer than 3 times in the night, then you may have XYZ in the morning. But, if you leave bed more than 3 times then you may not have XYZ." Over a given period, fade the number of times the child will be allowed out of bed and still be able to access the reinforcer.

The target figure will be determined based on the number of times the child is engaging in "out of bed" behavior at baseline (e.g., if it's 13, you might decide to reinforce 12 or less; if it's 6 times you might reinforce 5 or less). Raise the expectations as the child meets with success.

You will then fade reinforcement over time (e.g., they will stay in bed 2 consecutive nights to receive the reinforcer), until the child is sleeping in his own bed with nothing more than social reinforcement from you.

For a child who will not remember a delayed reinforcement contract, you might want to create a visual aid to explain reinforcement. One idea might be to have an = sign. On one side of the = is a picture which shows Johnny sleeping in bed, on the other side a picture of Johnny's highly preferred item. Place this by his bed as part of the bedtime routine. In the morning, if the goal is achieved, show him the visual and deliver the reinforcer.

Remember that your child may lose interest in the previously identified reinforcer as time goes along. In other words, he may become satiated on that particular reinforcer. Watch for this and be prepared to change reinforcement so that your child remains motivated.

Another sleep problem intervention is called Faded Bedtime with Response Cost (Piazza & Fisher, 1991). This approach aims to decrease the time between putting your child to bed and when they fall asleep (latency to sleep) to 15 minutes. You achieve this by keeping the child up past their typical bed time and then gradually fade back to the desired bed time over subsequent evenings.

To begin, identify the time your child actually falls asleep and then add 30 minutes. This becomes the new bedtime (e.g., you put your child to bed at 8pm and they fall asleep at 10:00 p.m., so you set their new bedtime for 10:30 p.m.). For the first night, keep the child out of bed until 10:30 p.m., by engaging with them in low-key play and attention. Don't allow them to fall asleep or to take a nap. If, when you put them to bed at 10:30 p.m., they fall asleep within 15 minutes, then the next night put them to bed 30 minutes earlier (e.g., 10:00 p.m.). If they do not fall asleep within 15 minutes then the next night add 30 minutes to the bedtime (e.g., 11:00 p.m.). Once they are falling asleep within 15 minutes, systematically and gradually fade back toward their ideal bed time by 30 minute increments (e.g., 10 p.m., 9:30 p.m., 9:00 p.m., etc.).

While this approach may seem counter-intuitive, it makes a great deal of sense from a learning standpoint. Right now, bed is not a signal for sleep. Your child is going there and is not falling asleep and thus bed is not associated with sleep. By not taking the child to bed until sleep is very likely, you are making that bed a signal for sleep the same way you suddenly feel like you have to eliminate whenever you enter a restroom.

The Response Cost comes into play when, having followed this method, your child wakes in the night. Require they stay up for 30 to 60 minutes (depending on parental preference and age of child) and do not allow them to access bed in that time (Ashbaugh & Peck, 1998). They may access toys and have your attention, but if they indicate fatigue do not allow access to bed until the time has expired. Research has shown that these "out of bed" occurrences decrease and "staying in bed" behavior increases simultaneously with fading the bedtime back to the desired time (Piazza & Fisher, 1991).

I have observed success with a combination approach. That is, I've combined Faded Bedtime with Planned Ignoring rather than Response Cost. As described above, determine the time your child actually falls asleep after you've put them to bed (e.g., child is put to bed at 8 p.m. but doesn't fall asleep until 9:30 p.m. Bedtime for the first night becomes 10 p.m.). Observe whether or not the child falls asleep within 15 minutes. Dependent upon the answer, subtract or add 30 minutes onto the bed time for the next night.

As previously mentioned, the first time the child leaves their bed, parents give one explanation, such as "It's bedtime, back to bed" as they lead the child back to bed with no further discussion, eye contact, or cuddles. Then, each subsequent "out of bed" behavior is treated similarly except this time there is no vocal explanation given. Again, the parent is ignoring the crying, vocal and physical protests, and negotiations.

No matter which procedure or combination of procedures you choose, peace can be regained. Give it a try and reclaim your sleep, your space and your privacy. Good luck and good night.

Chapter Ten

From Tantrums to Triumphs: Tackling the "Poo Problem"

Michelle Furminger

Toilet training for children with autism has been widely researched (e.g., Bettison, 1982; Dunlap, Koegel, & Koegel, 1984). The majority of research, however, has focused more on bladder control than on bowel control. There are many books and manuals on the market to help parents and caregivers to toilet train their child with autism, but most of this information addresses mastering urination in the toilet, rather than bowel motions. Many children are successful in gaining control of their bladder, but a common theme that seems to occur with families is how to tackle the "poo problem." This has not been addressed as much in the literature and many parents are at the end of their tether regarding how to fix it. Because of this, children with autism may need a separate bowel training program to tackle this issue.

Some children with autism pick up bowel control around the same time as bladder control, but, at least as often, this does not happen. This could be due to the fact that most children do not have a bowel motion as often as they urinate (thus fewer practice opportunities). It is also harder for parents and the therapist to manipulate the environment to ensure that the child moves his/her bowels more often. With training for bladder control, you can give your child copious amounts of liquid at a regular time interval (Bettison, 1982); you cannot easily do the same for bowel control. Past studies (e.g., Bach & Moylan, 1975; Butler, 1977; Crowley & Armstrong, 1977; O'Brien, Ross, & Christophersen, 1986) have found that use of suppositories and positive attention from family to be effective in tackling the problem, especially if the child is consistently constipated.

Sometimes, the "poo problem" is not due to the fact that the child is constipated, but rather due to other factors that may be influencing their behavior. A functional analysis should be administered to look at the function of the behavior that is maintaining the "poo problem." Does the child hide, ask for a nappy (Australian word for diaper), or do they smear their feces once they have had a bowel motion? Many children will avoid the toilet entirely and opt for doing their "number 2's" in private. This is usually not in the bathroom, but may be in a particular area of the house (like in the corner of the lounge room beside the sofa, by the sandpit, or between the fridge and the pantry in the kitchen). They may also prefer to have the comfort of a nappy to "do their business," rather than going to the bathroom and watching it flush away down the toilet.

Other environmental variables that need to be examined include how often the child goes, and what is a "regular" bowel motion for them. For some, this could be every day, every second day, or twice a day. The time of day that their bowel motions occur can play an important factor in solving the "poo problem" as well. Some will only go when they are asleep or after a meal. An additional variable to keep in mind is the latency of the behavior. This is a very important factor in toilet training. How soon does the child void after the "poo" signs are present? Latency data will tell you this.

Some individuals may have a very rigid behavior pattern towards their toileting ritual and if that is interrupted, there may be some tantrums or other challenging behaviors that may follow. So what could one do to solve this issue? To start with, before you tackle the "poo problem," it's important that the child has mastered bladder control, as bowel motions do not occur as frequently. Once this is achieved, start to think about the fact that having a bowel motion in the toilet is just like any other behavior. We need to look at the antecedent (what occurs before the behavior), as well as the consequence (what occurs after it). Are there particular signs that the child exhibits before they start their "poo ritual" that may help us identify when the child is going to have a bowel motion? We must also consider how we behave after the fact. Do we react in a particular way that may be maintaining the behavior (i.e., accidentally reinforcing the behavior with our reaction)?

The following discussion will go through 4 common "poo problems" that seem to occur in many of my consults. Each case will identify the antecedent behaviors, as well as the consequent behaviors. I will now address how we tackled each "poo problem" in detail.

Case 1: The boy who would hold forever

Adam was 4 years old at the time of consultation. He had a diagnosis of high functioning autism and was attending a mainstream preschool. He was toilet trained for his bladder and would take himself to the toilet when he needed to go. When it came to bowel motions, however, he would request a nappy and would void in it immediately. He would go into his room, put on his nappy, have a bowel movement, take it off and empty it in the toilet and go back to his previous activity.

Mum wanted Adam to be successfully trained to do bowel motions in the toilet because it was affecting their life (especially Adam's, as he was so anxious regarding this issue). Adam attended a mainstream preschool and he was the only child that wasn't fully toilet trained. She came and saw me around Christmas time for an initial consult and we put a plan together. We were going to throw away all the nappies so Adam couldn't request them. We also talked about finding a big tangible reinforcer to have in the bathroom, ready to go contingent on voiding in the toilet. Unfortunately, as it was Christmas time, the toileting procedure took a back seat (as it's our summer break over here and we have 6 weeks off). The family went away and the mum decided to tackle it once they got back.

The program started 3 months later. Mum took away the nappies, but progress was not instantaneous. Adam started to void in his underwear and bed. He had also started to hold in his bowel motions (as mum no longer had nappies in the house). As a very strong reinforcer was needed, Mum identified a Console game that Adam hadn't seen but knew that he would love. This was set aside to be given to him, contingent upon voiding in the toilet.

Adam's mum showed him the reinforcer and explained to him that he could play with this once he had had a bowel motion in the toilet. Adam understood this and would sit on the toilet. But as soon as he started to feel the urge to eliminate, he would get very anxious and would hold it all in. After 2 days of holding on, Adam was given a suppository in the morning to help move things along and to make it harder for him to hold it in. Mum put Adam back on the toilet. The chemist told us that this treatment would work within 15 minutes, but Adam was still fighting the urge to go. By lunchtime, 4 hours after the suppository was inserted, Adam still hadn't gone. He was given another suppository just after lunch to see if things would start moving this time. An hour later, Adam released the smallest bowel motion in the toilet (it was the tiniest drop). Because he voided something (even though it was really small) he was rewarded with a 10 minute break away from the toilet. Once the time had elapsed, Adam had to sit back on the toilet and focus on the job. Mum was doing the job, and at 4.30 p.m. I received a text that read, "Plop.... Plop...Plop...... SUCCESS!!!" Hurray! I was so happy for her! Adam got to play with his game console and mum got to relax and celebrate with a glass of champagne.

Two days later, it was déjà vu where Adam was refusing to go again, but mum followed through and used the same procedures that she used two days earlier and he went within 3 hours. Since then, Adam has been voiding in the toilet consistently. His success has maintained.

Case Study 2: The boy who would have accidents at home but not at school

Daniel was 5 years old at the time of consultation. He has a diagnosis of autism and attended a mainstream primary school. His mother came and saw me for a consult as Daniel was having numerous bowel motion accidents at home, but wasn't having any at school. After gathering some history of Daniel's toileting behavior, it was found that he was originally doing very well at home until he started school. Once he started school, he used to have a large number of accidents (both urination and bowel accidents) and he needed to be changed frequently at school. This year, though, Daniel seemed to have done a flip with his toileting behaviors and was now only having accidents at home.

From information gathered from Daniel's teacher and parents using a baseline data sheet, it was noted that Daniel didn't request to use the toilet at all. At home he would take himself, and at school he would wait until it was lunch or recess time to go. When Daniel did have an accident, the consequences were different in school than they were at home. At school, the teacher would calmly say to him, "Daniel, you are dirty, go to the toilet and clean yourself up." If Daniel had an accident at home, the consequence was more negative: "Oh no, not again, Daniel!" He also tended to do his bowel motions in his underwear and would be in a standing position with his legs apart when pushing.

Armed with this information, we collected bowel motion data for Daniel's toileting behavior for the next 9 days. Data collected included the time of the bowel motion, and what activity Daniel was engaged in when he went. Daniel's parents were told that if they saw that he needed to go, to redirect him to the bathroom to do his bowel motions and to close the door behind them (so he had some privacy). If they missed the opportunity to redirect him, they were to note which room he was in when he voided. If he did soil his pants, the parents were told to keep a neutral face and tell him to "clean it up" and prompt him to go and change his pants. They were also told to not get angry at Daniel or say it in an angry voice but instead to try and keep their voices and faces neutral (mirroring the precedent from the more currently successful setting). Once Daniel was changed, he could go about what he was doing previously before he had his accident. If Daniel initiated going to the toilet to do a bowel motion, he received a great deal of attention and reinforcement.

During data collection over the 9 days, Daniel started to tell people when he needed to do a bowel motion and was happy to be redirected to the bathroom to do it (more comfortable than the standing position he was in outside the bathroom). This was a good sign. Now that Daniel was happy to void in the bathroom standing (and not in other rooms of the house); he was prompted to sit each time he went to the toilet for both urination and bowel motions he could have some success with the bowel motions in the toilet. Daniel's requesting to go to the toilet was being targeted as well, for two reasons. The first reason was to reinforce the request and the second reason was that the parents were able to reinforce each success, as he told them that he needed to go (as opposed to when he took himself and no one knew if he actually did anything).

After looking at the baseline data, a bowel motion program was implemented. The program consisted of the following aspects: if Daniel requested to go to the toilet to urinate, he would be given his Lego car as a reward for requesting and he was prompted to sit on the toilet whilst urinating. If he did urinate in the toilet whilst sitting, he was then rewarded with access to a favored DVD. If Daniel requested to do a bowel motion in the toilet, he was given his Lego car for requesting and if he sat and did his bowel motion in the toilet, he was given access to dad's car (he loved just sitting dad's car and listening to the radio). If Daniel went to stand to do his bowel motions (as this was the position that he was in when he had his accidents), he was prompted to sit on the toilet seat using physical guidance.

If Daniel requested after he had already had an accident, then his mum or family members would redirect him to the toilet to change his pants while maintaining a poker face and making sure that any verbal instruction that was given to him was done with a neutral voice. Daniel did not get access to dad's car if he had soiled his pants, but he still got access to the Lego car for requesting for a bowel motion. His parents were also told that if Daniel attempted to take himself off to the toilet without requesting, they were to block access to the bathroom and prompt him to say, "I need to go to the toilet," and then let him go immediately. Daniel did not get the Lego car for this, as he did not independently request to go. When Daniel either urinated or had a bowel motion whilst sitting down, then he would get access to his big reinforcer (Dad's car for bowel motions or DVD for urinations done sitting). If he soiled his pants, no reinforcer was delivered for requesting or for voiding in his pants or standing up for urination. When Daniel needed to have a bowel motion, he would stand and lean against the arm of the lounge. If this was observed and he had not requested to go, Daniel was prompted to say, "I need to go to the toilet" and was redirected to the toilet using physical guidance (not verbal prompts) to sit on the toilet. If he voided with a bowel motion in the toilet while seated, he got access to Dad's car for 10 minutes but did not get access to the Lego car (as he did not request).

After a few days of intervention, Daniel started to consistently have his bowel motions in the toilet after gaining access to his favorite Lego car and Dad's car 3 times. These reinforcers were gradually faded out, using a fixed schedule, and he is now able to initiate requests for the toilet at home and at school without any accidents.

Case 3: The boy who would smear his feces

William, a 4 year old diagnosed with autism, was enrolled in an ABA program at the time of consultation. He initially had trouble with toileting when training for bladder control, as he would hold during his therapy session times and would have accidents after or between sessions (William was put back in a nappy as there was no one present to follow through with the consequence of redirecting him to the toilet if he voided). Baseline data were collected for a couple of weeks and showed that William would hold out to do his bowel motions until he was given a nappy. If William did have a bowel motion in his underwear or in his nappy, he would then smear feces all over himself. The consequence for the smearing was that his mum (his favorite person) would have to put him in the bath immediately and clean him up. William's antecedent signs for a bowel motion seemed to be when he played in the sandpit, stood next to the lounge with his legs apart, or stood next to the laundry door with his legs apart. William tended to smear during the busiest times of the day, when mum was cooking dinner and had to attend to the other children. By William smearing his feces and making a mess, this meant that mum had to stop attending to the other children and dinner to go and clean him up (lots of one-on-one attention!)

Based on this information, a bowel motion program was implemented. The program consisted of someone being with William the entire time. As mum was highly reinforcing to him, accidents did not lead to attention from mum and she would no longer take him to be cleaned if he smeared. A junior therapist on William's team would stay back after the sessions to be on "patrol" during those busy times of the day. Whilst on patrol, if they saw the antecedent signs (playing in the sandpit, standing next to lounge with legs apart, or standing next to laundry door with legs apart), they would immediately go up to him and say, "STOP! Toilet time," and immediately prompt him to the toilet using physical guidance. William had to remain seated on the toilet until 5 minutes had elapsed or he had completed his bowel motion. If William started his bowel motion in his pants, the therapist would still say, "STOP! Toilet time," and take him to the toilet. If William completed his bowel motion in the toilet, he still got access to his reinforcer. His reinforcer was mum's attention with a tangible reinforcer. This was originally chocolate, but this quickly changed to a big new flashing toy. The person on patrol had to clean William up if there he had an accident in his pants or if he smeared. He was immediately put in the shower by the therapist and cleaned up quickly. During this time, there was no eye contact or verbal interaction from the therapist. Mum did not come in and give William any attention when he had an accident. Instead, she would come in and give him lots of attention and reinforcement if he *did* have a bowel motion on the toilet.

After William's first bowel motion on the toilet and immediate access to mum and the chocolate, his 2 favorite things at that time, William started going up to mum to request for her to come to the toilet with him when he wanted to do a bowel motion. The therapist had to only clean up a smeared accident twice in 3 days and from then on there were no more smearing occurrences. William started to request independently and has not had accidents since. Maybe we shouldn't have called them accidents in the first place, since they were so clearly goal-directed, but you know what I mean.

Case Study 4: The boy who would only do a bowel motion when he was asleep

Max, who was diagnosed with autism, had just turned 4 when he came in for a consultation. His parents had been trying to toilet train him since he was 2 and a half years old. He was successfully trained for urination, and would sit on the toilet to urinate, but refused to sit on the toilet when a bowel motion was needed. Max would hold in his bowel motions until he was given a pull-up. Max was in his underwear all day, but would wait until he received his bedtime pull-up to have a bowel motion. He would only have a bowel motion if he was wearing a pull-up. If he needed to do a bowel motion during waking hours, Max would go and request for a pull-up. The antecedent sign for a bowel motion was to request for a pull-up, then go and hide in a room upstairs to eliminate (any room that did not have anyone present in it or in the bathroom).

Max also had a tendency to hold for a continuous number of days and was often constipated. His diet was quite restricted and he didn't eat a great deal of fiber or drink water frequently. Because of these factors, his parents and therapists worked on increasing Max's fiber intake and liquid consumption. They also recorded the time the pull-up went on and then the time Max took himself to a room to hide and have a bowel motion (latency).

The baseline data showed that the bowel motions started to occur during the night, while he was asleep. Because of this, a separate program was put in place to work on getting the bowel motions to occur during waking hours. The way we brought the bowel motions back into the waking hours was to give Max the pull up earlier in the day. We initially started to give it to him one hour before bed, but he still continued to go whilst he was asleep. So each day, we would give Max the pull up half an hour earlier than the day before and we started to be successful in getting the bowel motions to occur during waking hours (we found that if we gave him a pull up at 4 p.m., he would go late afternoon/early evening). The theoretical rationale is similar to that mentioned in the earlier chapter on sleep. Just as we want the bed to signal the body to sleep in that earlier example, so it was that the pull-up was signaling for bowel motions to occur.

Now that the bowel motions were occurring during waking hours, we were able to conduct the program that would result in the elimination of the pull-up. The procedure was as follows: a person would observe Max during the late afternoon time when he was in a pull-up. They would stand close to him (but not hover over him) when he was in his pull-up. This was so they could observe the antecedent signs (going to hide in a different room away from everyone and making pushing noises).

A pull-up was presented to Max at 4pm. The time the pull up went on to the time that he voided took an average of 45 minutes. If Max started to show the antecedent signs, the observer would come up to Max and say, "Stop, toilet," and redirect him to the toilet using physical guidance. No verbal prompts were used after the "Stop, toilet" was presented. This was so Max was not distracted by any verbal cues and could focus on voiding in the toilet. Max sat on the toilet until he voided or until 5 minutes were up, whichever occurred first. A special reinforcer was delivered to Max, contingent on a successful bowel motion in the toilet.

As Max was constantly constipated, a doctor was consulted and he recommended the use of suppositories to try and keep him regular (and to get some extra practice!). We only used them 3-4 times over a 2 week period and this helped him have a bowel motion during waking hours consistently. Max started to take himself to the toilet once he was consistently receiving a reinforcer for every occurrence of a bowel motion in the toilet. He then started to request to go when he was out of the home environment.

During the school holiday break, Max had one slip during his toilet training procedure. This was because reinforcers for bowel motions in the toilet were faded quickly, perhaps too quickly, to praise only. Realizing the mistake, we then changed his reinforcers to train trips (as they lived right next door to the train station) and paired it with a primary reinforcer (chocolate) and then he started to have bowel motions in the toilet again. The train trips were faded to just the chocolate, paired with praise, and eventually faded to just praise alone. Max now independently has bowel motions in the toilet during waking hours.

From the 4 case studies presented, it is important to note that each child is different and an individual program is required to be tailored to each child, dependent on behavioral function. Careful data collection, and altering procedures based upon those data, is key.

Chapter Eleven

The Case Against Sexual Behaviors in a Public School Environment

Cristiane B. Souza Bertone

It was my first year as a public school teacher in a self-contained classroom in New York. I was excited to inherit a classroom of 9 students, moving up from elementary school to middle school. All of the students had a diagnosis of autism spectrum disorder. I had not had any access to their records until the day of their arrival. The classroom staff informed me that these were "difficult children" and that I should "expect the worst." At that time, I was in the process of working on my certification in behavior analysis and I figured: "At least now I will be able to apply the theories I am learning." Despite having tremendous enthusiasm, emotional stamina, and determination, I was certainly not prepared for what lay ahead.

In this chapter I will be discussing the case of an adolescent diagnosed with autism during that first year of teaching. All the names and school locations are changed for confidentiality purposes. All the interventions were implemented under the supervision of an expert in the field of behavior analysis and sexuality (Thank you, Bobby!). The family was directly involved in the treatment (to you, Mr. and Mrs. B., thank you for believing in my work and for spending endless hours in meetings and implementing procedures!). And, finally, I must happily report that many lives were changed in the process . . . for the better.

Andrew was a 12-year-old male with an infectious smile. His levels of energy were higher than expected. To be more specific, he could easily run for over 4 hours without even breaking a sweat. He absolutely loved learning, but got bored easily. He needed a number of behavior support techniques to help him to stay on task and to socially and academically navigate the school environment. He was assigned a shared aide throughout the school day. Andrew was transitioning from one school building, where he had attended elementary school since age 5, to a different building where he was to attend middle school until he reached 16 years of age. Andrew adjusted well to the new classroom environment, new teacher, and new staff.

Life was going smoothly for Andrew until November, when he suddenly went through a growth spurt accompanied by a hormonal explosion. That was when he realized how great it felt to touch himself at any time and any where, started to run through the school hallways and classrooms (while they were in session), and finally tried to kiss an elderly man on the mouth at a local sandwich shop, while simultaneously trying to steal his milkshake. As I discussed earlier in the chapter, Andrew was diagnosed with autism. Due to his diagnosis, Andrew presented difficulties learning easily from the natural environment. Therefore, unspoken rules were non-existent in his world. He lacked the basic social skills to understand how important it is to respect boundaries and how to behave according to the school and community rules and expectations.

I communicated daily with his mother, who also worked with special needs students. We exchanged data regarding frequency, duration, and topographies of behaviors across home, school, and the community. Within a week of discussions, I observed that the challenging sexual behaviors were increasing in frequency and we both agreed that something had to be done immediately. Andrew was touching himself, gyrating, and rubbing his genitalia against furniture, more frequently by the day. He had not yet attempted to undress in public, but I did worry that without an intervention, the behaviors could escalate and this would also occur. I planned on conducting a functional behavior assessment and developing a functional behavior plan in order to modify the challenging behaviors and to replace them with appropriate behaviors.

Thinking back, under such circumstances I could not have wished for a better parent to work with. She understood the seriousness of the situation and she was quick to act. On that same evening, over one of many discussions, she gave me permission to discuss the case with my BCBA mentor, and to proceed with assessment and treatment of Andrew's inappropriate behaviors.

I went to Bobby's office for my regular supervision visit and shared my concerns about Andrew with him. I explained to him how I feared the situation could spiral out of control if anything happened outside the classroom and I asked for advice about how address the situation to help Andrew to sustain appropriate sexual behaviors in an appropriate setting. We discussed some theories, shared some ideas, and he offered me some literature on the subject of adolescence and sexuality. He also suggested that I look into the work done by Dr. Peter Gerhardt, another expert in the field. I could not find case studies published in peer review journals pertaining to the issue, but I was fortunate to have the best support currently available to me.

The very next day, as I got ready to begin my assessment, Andrew ran out of the classroom, stormed into a general education social studies classroom, grabbed a globe that was on the teacher's desk, threw it against the wall, jumped, screamed, laughed, and ran back to our classroom. I could not stop Andrew and all I remember was running after him and trying to redirect him while apologizing to the teacher and to the students for Andrew's challenging behaviors. When we finally made it back to our classroom, Andrew laughed hysterically, clapped his hands excitedly, had an erection, and pulled down his pants and touched himself. All of these behaviors happened in front of staff, teachers, and students who had never witnessed an adolescent diagnosed with autism experience what I would like to call a "hormonal rush." My heart was heavy with fear of what would come next. I verbally directed him to pull his pants up and walk to a cubicle area where he would be safe from the eyes of the horrified staff. He laughed throughout the process. He continued to touch himself while sitting at the desk and I continuously directed him to put his hands on the table. Within minutes, word got out about the events and in less than an hour I was called into the office by one of the school administrators. Luckily, at that time, Andrew was calmer and engaged in an academic task with a staff member.

During this meeting, an administrator questioned me about the student's behavior. If you think that managing Andrew's behavior was difficult, trying to explain to an administrator who was oblivious regarding autism, about what had just happened and why it had happened! I was informed that the best consequence would be to suspend Andrew from school until his behaviors were under control. I disagreed and explained that it was critical that we maintained him in school while providing all the supports necessary to teach him appropriate behavior. The administrator said he would have to discuss the matter with the director before making a final decision. Upon returning from the meeting, I called Andrew's mother immediately. I said, "They want him out of here. We need to do something." She immediately contacted the director of special services to also try to explain how critical it would be for us to work as a team. The director suggested we meet with the school psychologist to discuss the matter later that day. That evening, at 6 o'clock, Andrew's mother, the school psychologist, and I met in my classroom to discuss what would be the future of this child.

At the meeting, Andrew's mother shared all the behaviors she had observed around the community, including Andrew trying to kiss an elderly man at a local sandwich shop. We shared our data with the school psychologist. I explained that it was critical, due to my lack of experience with the situation, that the school allow an expert on adolescence and sexuality to join the team to help us in addressing this matter. After much discussion, the school psychologist promised to address our concerns with the school administration.

The administration agreed to allow Andrew to stay in school, as well as hire a consultant to teach us and train us on how to address Andrew's developmental issues. Andrew was, however, banned from the school cafeteria and any other areas used by other students throughout the school day. He was only allowed to stay in the classroom with myself and two staff members at all times.

Bobby arrived for the first visit. After analyzing the data, he instructed us that every time we observed Andrew initiating touching himself, we were to verbally redirect him to stop touching himself by teaching him to fold his hands. A time when he would be allowed to engage in self-touching behavior under appropriate conditions at home would have to be established. We also customized a story to teach Andrew the rules and expectations in school. Andrew was not too excited about the intervention, and, every time I intervened, his words to me were "not nice" before bursting into tears. His parents were in charge of closely supervising his behaviors at home and in the community. Andrew's father taught him how to appropriately have "me time" at home in his bedroom behind closed doors. This was not an easy process, but those were our only options.

Before the intervention, during our weeklong baseline, Andrew's inappropriate touching spiked from 14 to 36 times a day. Within a week of the intervention, Andrew was attempting to touch himself in school only once. Within two weeks, there were zero occurrences. At home, his father worked with him incidentally teaching him how to behave in order to properly address his sexual behavior within the privacy of his bedroom. He seized every opportunity of attempted inappropriate touching and taught him how, when, and where Andrew could engage in the behaviors. The parents reported that, along with a reduction of inappropriate touching in school, they observed that Andrew was spending more time in the evenings behind closed doors, likely engaging in more appropriate sexual behaviors (like many teens we could all probably name!).

The teaching period lasted approximately six weeks. The intervention was systematically faded to establish that Andrew had acquired the skills. After six months, we conducted a follow-up and we observed that Andrew had not only learned to control his sexual urges in school, but he also generalized the behavior across different environments. It is important to note that he was not allowed to perform the behavior anywhere but in his bedroom. Someone asked us why we would not allow him to touch himself while locked in a stall in the school too. To that question I replied: "Because we don't want him to do it at any other public restroom. He may generalize the idea of doing it in bathrooms and I really don't want that happening in the bathroom at the theater or football stadium!"

Andrew is now 15 years old. Through his hard work, as well as that of his family and the teaching staff, he has learned to behave appropriately and this, in turn, has allowed him to be more integrated in school activities and in the community. He continues to make strides both academically and behaviorally as he goes through adolescence, but many days still come with a challenge. Still, he has been able to successfully participate in two school trips, staying a total of two weeks away from home with two groups of general education students. People always refer to him as "awesome," "great student," "good listener," and "the life of the party." He continues to be a cheerful, fun, active teenager who lives his life to the fullest. He is learning that there are rules in life, however, and the better he understands them, the more likely he is to succeed.

Sexuality can be an uncomfortable subject for many parents and professionals. During the past 10 years of working in the field, I have heard many parents say that their special needs children do not have sexual needs and would never be able to express themselves sexually. According to research and literature, individuals diagnosed with disabilities do not necessarily have a sexual impairment. It is imperative to take a proactive attitude and consider that individuals diagnosed with disabilities are likely to present inappropriate sexual behavior if we do not provide proper guidance and instruction. This could expose them to dangerous social situations and make them more vulnerable to predators who would take advantage of their disability. In addition, they can be, and sometimes are, accused of criminal behavior due to society's failure to understand their natural inability to process its rules and behave according to the expectations. It is vital that we are proactive and provide our students with sexual education. By providing them with the right information and instruction, we are improving their quality of life and increasing their chances for a happier future.

Chapter Twelve

Teaching Functional Communication: If It's Not Broken, Why Fix It?

Elizabeth McAllister

A mother and father are sitting down after a long day to relax, unwind, and watch some television. Just as they are getting comfortable, their three-year-old daughter starts screaming. Alarmed, they rush upstairs and into her room. She sits perfectly well and unharmed on the edge of her bed and asks for a cookie and a glass of milk. Why didn't she simply come downstairs and ask for this snack? She clearly has the skills necessary to ask appropriately. The answer lies in her learning history. This precocious preschooler has learned that when she screams in her bedroom, her parents (naturally) come running and she doesn't have to leave the comfort of her bed. She has learned that she gets the cookie when she screams, and she gets it quickly. Therefore, screaming is a behavior that is extremely effective for her. Why would she fix a system that isn't broken?

Autism is characterized by deficits in communication, social skills and by repetitive, restricted interests (American Psychiatric Association, 1994). Individuals with autism sometimes exhibit problem behaviors such as destructive behavior (e.g., throwing objects), self-injurious behavior (SIB), and aggression towards others. As parents and caregivers, the key questions to ask when such behaviors occur are, "What function are these behaviors serving?" and, "Why is this child using that particular behavior?" The critical point to remember is that the behaviors are persisting because they are working; they are effective for the child. Our job is to first determine what function these problem behaviors are serving and then to teach appropriate, functionally equivalent alternative behaviors. We can teach our children to appropriately communicate their wants and needs only when they see that this approach works just as well, in fact, better, than the screaming or other problem behavior.

For each person, these inappropriate behaviors could be accomplishing one or multiple goals, depending on the context: escaping demands, accessing tangibles, gaining social attention, or providing automatic reinforcement (Iwata, Dorsey, Slifer, Bauman & Richman, 1994). In order to teach functional communication, it is important to determine what function the behavior is currently serving. The following hypothetical scenarios, which use elements from my clinical practice, provide examples of problem behaviors serving each of the four functions listed above, along with behavioral solutions that would reduce or eliminate the inappropriate behavioral tendency.

Escape from demands

Jim is a five-year-old, nonverbal boy diagnosed on the autism spectrum. Jim sometimes throws objects at the people in his vicinity. Amy, his therapist, works with Jim several times a week. Amy starts writing down the details each time Jim throws an object. She records what happened right before the throw (the Antecedent conditions), what the Behavior looked like, and what happened right after the behavior (the Consequence). Amy is taking ABC (Antecedent-Behavior-Consequence) data (a type of functional assessment) to develop hypotheses regarding Jim's throwing behavior. Behavior analysts may also choose to perform a functional analysis, in which conditions are experimentally manipulated, to determine the function of a particular behavior (Iwata, et al., 1994). After taking data for several weeks, Amy notices a pattern. Before Jim throws an object, Amy is always in the process of initiating an academic demand, namely math work. As soon as Jim throws the object, Amy's attention is diverted away from the demand while she goes and picks up the object. Essentially, Jim's good arm has earned him a break from the proposed demand. His problem behavior efficiently provides him an escape from work. How can Amy decrease Jim's throwing behavior? She needs to provide Jim with an alternative behavior that will also earn him a break.

Jim wants to ask for a break, but lacks the communication skills to do so appropriately. Amy could teach Jim to hand her a communication card (labeled "break"). She would do this by errorlessly (hand-over-hand) prompting Jim to hand her the card as soon as math work was about to start. Once he gave her the card, she could give him a 30-second break before starting work again and would praise his appropriate communication. Amy would continue to prompt Jim to use the card at the onset of math work until he was spontaneously asking for breaks. Any throwing behavior would not remove the demand. Amy would simply leave the object where it landed and continue with the math work. This procedure is known as differential reinforcement of alternative behavior (DRA), as one behavior (using the card) is being reinforced, while the other behavior (throwing) is put on extinction (reinforcement is withheld). The important component of this procedure is that Jim is learning that by emitting an appropriate response of handing over a card, he is achieving the same results as when he was throwing objects, but now he is also earning social praise. For Jim, the value of the appropriate response is greater than that of the inappropriate response. Jim could also be taught that he could only request a break when the "break" communication card is available, thus preventing excessive breaks from instruction (Fisher, Adelinis, Thompson, Worsdell, & Zarcone, 1998). He could also be taught to ask for help with the task rather than to ask for a break, which would make the math demand less difficult and would make escape less valuable (Carr & Durand, 1985).

Accessing tangibles

Anna is a ten-year-old girl diagnosed on the autism spectrum, who loves her computer. She spends large amounts of time looking up her favorite games and videos on

YouTube™. When Anna wants her computer and her sister is using it, she will scream and pinch her sister until she gets off. At that time, Anna gets to use the computer. What alternative behavior could Anna be taught? Because Anna has some language, she could be taught to ask her sister, "I want computer," at which point she would gain access to her favorite activity. What if Anna couldn't have the computer at that time, as her sister needed it for school? Her communication should still be reinforced ("Great job asking for the computer, Anna! You can have your iPod while you are waiting.") and she could be shown in a picture schedule when she would gain access to the computer. Any screaming or pinching would not lead to access to the computer, or anything else reinforcing for that matter. Again, we are using the DRA procedure to teach Anna that appropriate behavior will help her access her favorite things and inappropriate behavior will certainly not.

Gaining social attention

Andrew is an eleven-year-old student diagnosed with ASD who attends a general education classroom. His teacher has thirty students in her classroom and her time with Andrew is generally very limited. Andrew has strong verbal skills. Several times a day, Andrew will reach out and hit the student to his right or left. At that time, his teacher will stop her interactions with the other students and will chastise Andrew, giving him her full attention. A functional analysis conducted by a behavior analyst revealed that Andrew only engages in this behavior to gain attention from his teacher, even though it might be considered unpleasant attention. We need to show Andrew how to gain his teacher's attention in a more socially acceptable way. Andrew could receive attention each time he put up his hand and said, "How is my work?" to which the teacher would respond with praise (Carr & Durand, 1985). Any hitting behavior would be ignored (placed on extinction). To protect the other students, the teacher could place Andrew's chair slightly out of reach of his neighbors, since he does not leave his desk to strike others. By teaching functional communication, Andrew's behavior is reinforced when he asks for social interaction instead of attempting to obtain it through aggression.

Accessing self-stimulatory reinforcement

Matthew is a sixteen-year-old diagnosed with autism who has some verbal abilities. His therapists notice that Matthew engages in low levels of self-injurious behavior (SIB) at various times throughout the day, including times of academic demands, low social attention, and when without favorite items. He also engages in SIB when he is completely on his own and accessing all his favorite things. His behavior analyst determines that because Matthew engages in the behavior across all contexts, it must serve an automatic reinforcement function – that is, the action itself is reinforcing. This scenario is different from our other students in a key way: Matthew's behavior is providing its own reinforcement, instead of our other examples in which reinforcement was delivered by others. Here we again need to provide a functionally equivalent alternative response. What else does Matthew find engaging that could compete with the SIB? We need to find items for Matthew to hold or keep his hands busy with that can compete with his SIB. We need to provide sufficient reinforcement for appropriate alternative responses, such as squeezing a stress ball or engaging in a preferred activity, so that the SIB maintained by automatic reinforcement is not as valued and therefore as likely. Competing reinforcers must be found for the self-injurious behaviors that are easily accessible for the student to ensure that Matthew chooses these reinforcers over SIB (Shore, Iwata, DeLeon, Kahng, & Smith, 1997). As was the case in our other scenarios, any reinforcer available at the time of the SIB should be removed, so that it is clear that these behaviors do not lead to access to preferred items.

By teaching appropriate behaviors that serve the same function as inappropriate behaviors, individuals with autism can learn to communicate successfully. By implementing behavioral treatment plans that address the function of the behavior, we can target the root of the problem. Returning to our opening example, how could those fatigued parents teach their daughter to come and ask for a cookie instead of screaming for a cookie? What if she learned that if she came downstairs and asked nicely, she could have a cookie and milk, but if she screamed from her room, she would have to wait until the following evening for her preferred snack? Do you think she would quickly learn to come down the stairs and ask for her cookie? I'm confident she would, as she would now be using a system that allows her to effectively communicate her wants and needs. And if the system isn't broken, why fix it?

Chapter Thirteen

Food Selectivity: The Next Frontier of Autism Research

Edward Vinski and Lauren Porter

Cathy Delmonico has prepared a large roast beef for her family's Sunday meal. When the family gathers for dinner, she prepares a plate of meat, potatoes, and vegetables for her daughter, Yvonne, who has autism. When the plate is put in front of Yvonne, the girl gently pushes it away. When it is replaced, she screams and knocks it to the floor. Cathy sighs and leaves the rest of her family at the table to prepare macaroni and cheese for Yvonne.

A core diagnostic symptom of autism is a pattern of restricted interests and repetitive behaviors. Changes in routine and novel experiences are often resisted by those diagnosed with the disorder. Many exhibit stereotyped behaviors that may present as hypersensitivity to various sensory experiences. One consequence of these symptoms is that persons with autism may exhibit food selectivity. For instance, they may reject trying new foods or refuse foods based upon, among other things, the texture, temperature, or olfactory characteristics of the food presented to them.

Several anecdotal studies describe children with autism spectrum disorders as exhibiting food selectivity (e.g., Ahearn, Castine, Nault, & Green, 2001). Although prevalence rates vary considerably, possibly due to a lack of objective and systematic studies in the area, food selectivity appears to be a common occurrence in children with ASDs. Rates from survey research range from 30% to as high as 90%.

Ahearn, et al. (2001) assessed food acceptance in 30 participants diagnosed with ASDs (i.e., autism and pervasive developmental disorder not otherwise specified). Over six sessions, foods from four categories (fruit, vegetable, starch, and protein) were presented to the participants for self-feeding. Data collectors categorized each behavior into one of three areas:

> *Acceptance* – picking up food with or without using a spoon, opening the mouth and placing food in the mouth.
>
> *Expulsion* – the food appeared past the border of the lip after food had been accepted (i.e., spitting or pulling the food out of the mouth).
>
> *Disruption* – any response that interrupted the presentation of food on the plate (e.g., batting at the plate or spoon after presentation).

The data collectors recorded the responses that occurred during each trial. Ahearn, et al. (2001) found that more than half of the participants exhibited low levels of food acceptance with only 13% exhibiting high level of acceptance. The same percentage of participants exhibited some level of food selectivity. While the authors admit to using a limited sample, this objective study represents an improvement over the traditional survey methods of obtaining prevalence information. It also indicates that food selectivity may occur in a majority of cases.

Clearly such feeding issues might lead to health consequences. For instance, Schreck, et al. (2004, as cited in Herndon, DiGuiseppi, Johnson, Leiferman, & Reynolds, 2009) found that children with ASDs took in fewer fruits and vegetables, starches and dairy products than did children in a control group. Herndon, et al. (2009) found that calcium intake was lower among children with ASDs than among controls, as was the consumption of dairy products. Although methodological issues often limit the extent to which the results of such research can be generalized, Herndon, et al. (2009) concluded that "pediatricians and parents of children with ASDs, especially children with dietary restrictions, need to be aware of the potential for nutritional deficiencies" (p. 221).

Fortunately, behavioral interventions have been shown to be particularly effective in treating food selectivity. One of the most thoroughly researched interventions is a procedure known as non-removal of the spoon (NRS). In this intervention, a bite of food is presented to the child. The spoon is then held directly in front of the child's mouth until he or she consumes the food. While this procedure has been demonstrated to be quite effective, there have been anecdotal reports that parents are troubled with its perceived intrusiveness (Tarbox, Schiff, & Najdowski, 2010).

Since the effectiveness of NRS appears to be based upon extinguishing an escape/avoidance response (i.e., removal of the demand to consume the food), it stands to reason that other procedures geared toward extinguishing that response would be similarly effective. Tarbox, et al. (2010) examined an intervention that not only appears to follow the extinction paradigm, but also is likely among the most commonly used parenting techniques when addressing mealtime behaviors: requiring that the meal be finished before the child is allowed to leave the table. As of this writing, this technique (which may be called "non-removal of the meal" or NRM) has not be extensively studied as an intervention for food selectivity. Preliminary evidence is encouraging, however.

Tarbox, et al. (2010) examined the efficacy of NRM through the case study of a 3 year old boy with autism named Ed. The child's mother reported that while his food selectivity/refusal was not extreme, it was a source of stress at the dinner table. She was also concerned that Ed's diet may not have been nutritionally adequate.

Ed's mother was responsible for following the intervention plan and collecting data on its effectiveness. The percentage of the meal consumed and the duration of the meal were recorded as dependent variables. During the baseline phase of the case study, Ed's meals followed their typical pattern with no consequences imposed for food acceptance or refusal. During the intervention phase, however, the child was informed that he would have to remain at the table if he did not finish the meal. Additionally, his mother told him that if he did not finish the meal by bedtime, he would have to eat it for breakfast the next morning. Following the intervention phase was a return to baseline phase to show that any changes in eating habits were, in fact, due to the intervention. After this, the intervention was reactivated.

During the initial baseline phase, the child consumed, on average, 29% of food per meal. The percentage of food consumed increased to 97% during the intervention phase. When the baseline phase was reinstituted, this percentage dropped to 17% before returning to 100% when the intervention was reinstated.

Although the average meal duration remained at approximately 30 minutes, the authors were encouraged by the results of an NRM approach to addressing food selectivity. The procedure offers several advantages, two of which we might mention. In the first place, it appears to be a common approach utilized by many parents, so it is not likely to be perceived as odd or intrusive. Second, it is a simple paradigm that does not involve complex details and steps to which parents must attend.

As has been indicated in this chapter, a great deal of research remains necessary before definitive conclusions can be drawn regarding food selectivity among children with ASDs. While the Tarbox, et al. case study's results must be interpreted and generalized with great caution, and while further objective and systematic research is needed to support the efficacy of NRM, it appears to be a simple, common-sense approach to addressing a behavior that is a source of great distress to the parents of children with autism.

Chapter Fourteen

Man Was Not Made for the Sabbath . . .

Susan Kenny

I'm going to come at this in a bit of a different manner from the other authors in this volume. I will be approaching things not from the perspective of a direct care clinician, as many of my co-authors are, but rather as a school administrator. My clinician colleagues have to consider not just accepting that a behavior is inevitable because a student is diagnosed with autism. In my role as administrator, I have to consider that just accepting rules or policy because it has always been that way may not be in the best interests of all students.

I was the principal at a public school where an intensive teaching program was housed. This program primarily served students diagnosed on the autism spectrum. As we were all to experience, sometimes that meant that we had to think about school rules a little differently. That guiding principle that teachers so often have to explore with their classes, "fair doesn't mean everyone gets the same thing," was never more evident.

Obviously, a school needs rules in order to function effectively. The rules are there for a reason, and they are there to make sure everyone stays safe and learns effectively. If I may paraphrase Dr. Seuss, however, "except when they don't." There were times when the school rules actually hindered the functioning of the intensive teaching class. And as the famous Biblical passage reads that "Man was not made for the Sabbath . . ." so we had to consider that the students were not made for the rules.

I believe my first confrontation with this important concept as regards the intensive teaching class came in my first meeting with the consultant for the program, my co-author Bobby Newman. I generally enjoyed the meetings with Bobby, as it was fun in that I never did know what the little maniac would hit me with next. Sometimes the requests did get a little out there!

What was funny about the initial meetings, however, was that Bobby would come armed with all kinds of data and arguments and legal precedents to try to convince me of things that I really didn't need to be convinced about. Maybe some of his prior administrators were a little less used to thinking outside the box, I don't know. It was almost funny, though, when Bobby asked me to make an exception to the school rule barring students from going on Youtube™. It seems that it was a very powerful reinforcer for some students in the intensive teaching class and he felt that it was absolutely essential to the success of some treatment plans that the students had access. He really seemed disappointed when I almost immediately told him that it seemed reasonable and the students in those classrooms could go on the closed sites, provided they were supervised in their content. I guess he was sad he didn't get a chance to use all his arguments!

We had many such discussions over the course of our time together. Another instance that comes to mind revolved around an upcoming field trip. The very excellent teachers in the intensive teaching program were determined that the students in their classes should not have to ride to the field trip on their own, smaller bus. They wanted the students to ride on the big bus with everyone else.

To do this, of course, would take some preparation. The first thing Bobby asked me for was a big bus and driver to do a few dry runs during the school day, where the students from the intensive teaching classroom would practice riding on the big bus. Then, he wanted to be able to "borrow" some hand-picked typically-developing students to ride on the bus with the students from the intensive teaching class to systematically increase the amount of noise and crowding that would be experienced. As usual, I think he was surprised that it wasn't such a big deal for me to arrange. Typically developing students came into the class to do reverse mainstreaming anyway; in this case we would just do it on the bus. It was what was necessary for student success, so we made it happen.

We could provide many such examples. Over the years, many such issues had to be addressed. General staff from the building needed time to be trained regarding how to not accidentally violate a treatment plan, and a mechanism telling them just what those treatment plans were needed to be designed. Staff needed time to be trained how to handle physical crises rather than just calling Bobby (nicknamed "911" in such cases) or another individual if he was not on campus. Provisions needed to be made for older students who needed assistance with menstrual care or the wearing of a bra. General staff were trained regarding behavior targets that they should be sure to reinforce, when they saw students behaving appropriately.

The list could go on. The key point remains the same. The rules of the school were good, and they were there to keep everyone safe and to maximize everyone's education. But to again return to our Dr. Seuss, except when they didn't, and that's when we had to reconsider. We watched the changes in the students, both in the intensive teaching class and in the typically-developing population that learned so much about themselves and the other students through their interactions. And it was very good.

Chapter Fifteen

We Can't Even Think of a Word That Rhymes:

Addressing Video Watching/Rewinding and Watching/Rewinding and Watching/Rewinding....

We'll begin with a bit of self-disclosure. I am a Muppet and Sesame Street fan from way back. I grew up with those characters, from the days before they were politically correct and when several of the characters had easily identifiable psychological disorders. I tried to never miss an episode, and truth be known, my son and I own every season of the Muppet Show on DVD, as well as some of their other "best of" DVDs. Among those is the classic "Alice Cooper as the guest star" episode that will factor into our current discussion.

For our current discussion, we will consider Kevin, a six year old boy diagnosed on the autism spectrum. I was asked to help to develop some programming to increase Kevin's independent spoken language. A behavior that was competing with independent language, however, was Kevin's tendency to echolate (repeat) particular phrases. One phrase that was particularly prevalent was familiar the first time I heard Kevin say it, but I couldn't immediately place it: "We can't even think of a word that rhymes!" Baseline data indicated he would say this phrase up to 10 times per minute, with rarely more than 2 minutes going by without him saying it.

I'm embarrassed to say that it took me a few seconds to remember the reference. It is, of course, from Alice Cooper's *School's Out*, and I hope you can agree it numbers among the best single lines ever to appear in a rock and roll song. I guess I was thrown off by Kevin's comparatively young age, compared to when that song was in the Top 40 (for you youngsters, I used to listen to it on a big, black vinyl CD that we called a "record").

The gap was bridged when I saw that Kevin enjoyed watching Alice perform the song, along with some extra large muppets, on the classic episode. As I mentioned, I had no problem with his choice of entertainment. My problem was that he only watched about 15 seconds of the video. Then he would rewind and watch those same 15 seconds, and then he would do it again, and then again. His parents informed me that left to his own devices, Kevin would do this for several hours at a time. The fact that he then repeated the line as often as he did was suddenly no mystery. Such perseverative video watching/rewinding is not an uncommon behavior among individuals diagnosed on the autism spectrum (although I do admit that I preferred Alice Cooper to the usual selection of *Thomas the Tank Engine* and *The Wiggles* I usually experience). Such perseverative watching, in turn, often leads to perseverative repeating of dialogue.

I asked if this behavior had been addressed previously, and Kevin's parents informed me that they had been telling him to stop. In an attempt to make this direction concrete, Kevin's father had even taken a hammer to the VHS recording in front of Kevin (for you youngsters: VHS tapes were like rectangular DVDs, made of plastic and tape). Unfortunately, this intervention was not effective, not to mention the fact that the video clip was available on internet sites, and Kevin partook freely.

In an attempt to begin to address this behavior, the first thing was obviously to interfere with the constant watching and rewinding of the clip. I didn't recommend eliminating the video entirely, as I saw the reinforcer value in it, but added a new requirement. If Kevin were to watch a video, he had to watch it ALL THE WAY THROUGH. There were also limits regarding how many times he could choose a single video to watch. We provided Kevin with a set number of tickets that could be used each day to "purchase" the video clip. That number of tickets was systematically decreased as we went.

To undertake this effort, supervision of video watching was necessary. Kevin needed to be monitored when he was on the television or computer, and power was cut off to the devices through a circuit breaker when Kevin could not be watched as closely (to prevent covert repeated watching/rewinding). During the monitoring, Kevin was allowed to watch his chosen video, but if he attempted to rewind the video to watch the same few seconds again, he was verbally redirected and, if necessary, physically blocked.

Kevin was, of course, not thrilled with the new arrangement when it was introduced. He engaged in some tantrum behavior, and, for a short time, he lost interest in watching videos. To ensure that the video watching stayed "on the radar," it was made into a reinforcer on his token board for work completion (prior, there had been noncontingent access). As a result, perseverative watching of his one video, or to be more specific the small clip from his one video, decreased. Echolation of the line then also decreased.

Watching a particular portion of a video is not an atypical behavior, whether we are talking about students diagnosed on the autism spectrum or typically developing students. If you have seen the "As God is my witness, I thought turkeys could fly," clip from the old television show *WKRP in Cincinnati*, you've probably played it multiple times for both yourself and your friends. Perhaps you have re-watched, and multiply forwarded by email, the Muppet version of *Bohemian*

Rhapsody. There's no problem there. Obviously, the problem is only when the behavior becomes obsessive and blocks out other activities.

Chapter Sixteen

Let There be an Object Lesson!

"Let there be an object lesson!"

Periodically, throughout my career, I have felt that I heard this phrase being said to me from some spiritual plane. Such was the case one afternoon at an afterschool recreational/educational program in the 1990's. One of the students who attended the program was James, a young man in his late teens who enjoyed shooting free-throws. That is actually a slight understatement. James was obsessive about free-throws and needed to sink 20 shots before he would leave the gymnasium.

James' obsessive behavior regarding the free-throws was well-known among the staff. It had not been made a priority, however, as he was well able to sink the requisite number of shots during the time his group was scheduled in the gymnasium. The fact that he was over six feet, five inches tall and could become physically aggressive when frustrated no doubt potentially played into this under-prioritization as well. All was well, why mess with it?

All was well, of course, until the "object lesson" day, that is. James had just made 13 of his 20 free-throws, and the fire drill alarm sounded. Everyone made an orderly move towards the exits, except James. He refused to leave the gym, much less leave the building, until he sank his 20 free-throws.

I ran through a quick series of prompts to attempt to get James to leave. He was having none of it. Finally, with nothing else to do, I began to physically escort James towards the door. We must have quite a sight, all six foot five of him, with all five foot five or six or me escorting him to the door. James made his displeasure known. He leaned down and sank his teeth into my left deltoid and refused to release.

It was one of those surreal moments in life that those who work with people who may engage in severely challenging behavior get used to, and then find it odd when others in their lives react with surprise ("You got vomited on?" or, "You got bitten?" or, "You got urinated on?"). In this case, we moved out of the building, the blood slowly running down my arm. As I looked over, all I could think of was my beloved father and his tendency to repeat stock phrases at such times. In this case, the stock phrase was, "Yeah, that's gonna leave a mark."

Leave a mark it did. My wife called it my *Raiders of the Lost Ark* scar. You could have made braces for James' teeth by examining the scar on my deltoid. I eventually covered it with what I hope is a nicer looking tattoo of an orca, but that's neither here nor there.

Obviously, the staff and I had put off addressing a crucial behavior problem for far too long. The fact that there might be circumstances in life where James' ritual might HAVE to be violated, whether we planned on it or not, had not been properly appreciated. To be more honest, it had probably just been avoided. We knew it would be unpleasant and had put it off.

The object lesson was learned. We needed to address the behavior. We began the Response Interruption procedure. The plan was basically as follows:

1. We would set up a situation wherein James would begin shooting his free-throws, but would not be allowed to sink all 20.

2. We would attempt to cushion the blow by teaching James some physical exercises to do when he began to feel agitated.

3. We prepared James at the beginning of each session regarding how many free-throws he would be allowed to sink before the session ended.

4. We attempted to leave an element of the ritualistic behavior intact by providing James with a "scorecard" that had slots for the set number of free-throws he would sink that day (e.g., 18 boxes to tick off as he sank 18 free-throws, or 15 boxes to tick off as he sank 15 free-throws). The idea here was that we were providing him with an opportunity to "complete" the activity, while still systematically varying the number of shots he would sink. Over time, we would attempt to fade this scorecard and introduce more competitive basketball.

5. Once James filled his card, the activity would end. We would all begin leaving the gym, taking the ball with us and prompting James to engage in behavior such as putting away equipment that was associated with "cleaning up."

James was clearly not happy about the new arrangements, but fortunately did not become physically aggressive. He gradually accepted the number of free-throws he would be allowed to sink each day, and then we let him choose his "goal" for the day. Once the number sank did not seem to be as crucial as it had been before, we attempted to change things further by interrupting James' shooting to ask him to do something else in the gym and then return to his free-throws. Following this, we interrupted and did not return to the court.

Object lesson learned by me. I hope next time I won't need someone to bite into me in order to get it.

Chapter Seventeen

Losing Control, Under Controlled Conditions

Stuff happens in life. A tire goes flat, there's an accident on the highway, an airplane is cancelled or delayed, a road is closed due to a flood. Sometimes we're late and there's nothing we can do about it. Such disappointments and frustrations are a part of life. For many students diagnosed on the autism spectrum, however, they seem to be much harder to handle than for the typically-developing population. It may be difficult to determine whether this is due to social or language difficulties that make it hard to comprehend the reason behind the delay, or because of obsessive-compulsive traits. Regardless of the reason, unexpected events may lead to lateness, and that causes some students diagnosed on the autism spectrum to become quite upset. In one extreme example, a father reported to me that his teenaged son, well over 200 pounds, used to choke him from behind if they were in the car and it was slowed in traffic.

Such violent outbursts are unacceptable, of course, and require that we design treatment plans to ensure that unavoidable delays in life are tolerated without behavioral explosions.

Let's consider Scott, a high school student who could not tolerate being late. He would attempt to leave one class early, in order to be at the next class on time. He would verbally perseverate regarding being late and how his teachers would be mad at him if he were late. Scott's behavior was extremely rule-governed, and he knew there were rules against lateness. He didn't want to break those rules.

Following the clue regarding the verbal perseveration about rules, Scott's behavior was more deeply examined. It was determined that this lateness obsession was part of a larger series of behaviors surrounding following the rules. He would also, according to his teachers, "fall apart" if he got an item wrong on his spelling test or forgot a line in his drama class. While everyone tried to assure him that "it's ok to make a mistake" and that such things were inevitable in life, Scott seemed to live in fear of such occurrences.

In order to begin addressing the behavior, we began examining our assets: Scott was very good at following rules. The suggested strategy, therefore, was to make "making a mistake" into a rule (I know it sounds paradoxical, but stick with me). A math worksheet was created for Scott, and he was informed that part of the exercise was to *deliberately* make a mistake. He could choose which example, and he could choose the nature of the mistake, but one of the answers had to be wrong. It was explained that this was a game with the teacher, and a second part of the assignment was going to be "finding and fixing" the mistake.

Note that the control stayed with Scott. He could choose where the mistake would be and what it would be. His teacher played it up, making a big deal out of it being a silly joke when the mistake was located, and then working on the skill of "find and fix." Scott enjoyed the game, and enjoyed the attention that came along with it. We were in a good place. The "rule" against having to hand in a perfect paper each time was being bent, if not completely broken.

Scott's teacher took a next step. She then made a class project of "find the mistake." Imperfect papers were stapled to the bulletin board, and other students (carefully coached to know it was a game and to never make fun of an error, but to rather congratulate the clever hiding of a mistaken answer) searched for the mistakes. Other students were brought in on the game, and they deliberately made mistakes and Scott found theirs. The teacher made a general policy of putting slightly imperfect papers up on the wall, even under "non game" conditions.

Through this game, Scott became less and less concerned with accidental errors. Of course, we needed to make sure that he did not deliberately make errors all the time, but that was just a matter of creating stimulus control. Assignments where an error was expected were clearly marked as such. Unfortunately, the results of this intervention did not generalize to the lateness issue. Scott was still very concerned with being late.

A similar strategy was employed to help with lateness. Teachers for the next class discussed with Scott when he would show up. He was given choices. He could be there "on time," "a minute early," "a minute late," "two minutes early," or "five minutes late." Scott had to choose among these options and arrive when specified, but he could not pick the same time slot repeatedly. He would have to be early sometimes and late sometimes. Again, it was with everyone's agreement and under Scott's control, but we were looking to chip away at the rigidity of always having to be on time. We decided to allow early as well as late to increase flexibility and further break down rigidity.

The strategy was successful. Over time, deliberate lateness that did not cause upset gave way to accidental lateness that did not cause upset. A teacher would deliberately/accidentally go a bit over her time, in order to create the opportunity to be late to the next class, once we were ready to practice "spontaneous" lateness.

The general moral of this story is to work with what you have. We had a student who was extremely anxious and dealt with that anxiety by always following the rules. Those rules said that you had to be perfect. Rather than attempt to change the student, we changed the rules. Then we faded them back to the regular rules, always under choice and control conditions that allowed for variation from routine, but without upset. We exposed Scott to what troubled him, but under conditions that allowed him to deal with that exposure.

Chapter Eighteen

"At My Most Cunning . . .": Considering Age-Appropriateness

In an earlier chapter, I pointed out that I am a huge Muppet and Sesame Street fan, particularly from before the toning down of their characters and from the days when James Coburn could smoke a cigar on The Muppet Show without causing a national crisis. It has been a lifelong goal of mine to appear with the Muppets, both as myself and as a Muppet performer.

That being said, I have to relate an incident that led to the title of this chapter. I had been asked to help a fifth grade student, diagnosed with autism, to join an academic class and social group with his typically-developing peers. The student in question, however, was dressed in a t-shirt that featured pictures of preschooler's television characters and he literally had no other cultural referents from which to make conversation. While things have changed considerably these days, at the point in our cultural history when this story took place, my spontaneous answer was, "At my most cunning, I couldn't think of a way to do this." At that point in our history, and within the sub-culture of the neighborhood in which I was working, neither of us stood a chance. It is one thing to be cute and occasionally wear a t-shirt with a cartoon character, particularly an edgy one such as Bugs Bunny or the Tasmanian Devil. It is quite another thing, at this student's age, to *only* be able to wear the clothing featuring the more babyish characters and to have nothing else to discuss with peers. In a worst case scenario, he would have been the target of bullying; in the best case scenario, he would have been having very patronizing interactions with his peers.

What was needed was an intensive round of "reinforcer sampling." The student in question, Mel, would have to be exposed to a variety of other media and learn to appreciate more age-appropriate materials.

To accomplish this, we began the use of a Premack Hierarchy (a more probable behavior, in this case watching his shows aimed at younger viewers, would be used to reinforce a lower probability behavior, in this case watching shows aimed more at his age-group). Shows that featured music and physical comedy were chosen, as this emphasis downplayed the more complex language that would have made understanding the plots of some other shows more difficult for Mel to follow. Parents and selected peers watched the shows along with Mel to try to keep his interest and to help him to appreciate the programs/characters.

It should be noted that in many such cases, all access to the material aimed at younger viewers must be eliminated. For some students, just a little access is not enough and they feel compelled to attempt to watch as much as possible and refuse all other options if their old show is available, even in lesser amounts. In Mel's case, however, we were able to show that he could tolerate less access to reruns of his favorite old shows, and we were happy with that because he was earning it by being exposed to the more age-appropriate material and clothing. Similarly, he was able to wear older, favored clothing (until he grew out of it) on non-school days.

Fortunately, this particular situation worked itself out well and with much less effort than is typically the case. Mel took to some of the new television programs, as well as their music, and developed some more age-appropriate cultural referents. We simultaneously made a push on other activities that were favored by his peer group, including sports and video-games. He took to the latter nicely, and a context from which to create appropriate peer interactions gradually formed.

It might seem harsh to not let Mel just "be himself" and wear and watch and discuss what he wanted to, even if it would be considered highly immature for his age by the population at large. There was certainly a part of me that felt that way. Why should Mel have to conform to existing societal norms? An argument could certainly be made for allowing him to "be himself."

In this case, however, I was not interested in an argument or in philosophical discussion. There was a great deal of fun, both in terms of experiencing new things and making relationships with peers, that were being severely hampered by Mel's age-inappropriate interests. The typically-developing peers would never have accepted these interests, and even if they did, Mel would never have been regarded as a peer but rather as a severely delayed individual. By developing the other interests, Mel was able to partake of much more that life had to offer, and he was still allowed to partake in the older activities in lesser amounts, until, eventually, *he didn't want to anymore*.

As alluded to above, there are times when the strategy that worked with Mel is not going to be effective. The student may resist all other options if their old choices are still available, even in small amounts. Or, they may continue to speak of nothing else and insist on the same clothing, even when exposed to new options. In such cases, exposure to the older material may have to be eliminated, at least for a time. This can introduce variations into the carrying out of programs.

Such was the case with one mother and son that I will now describe. The child in our story, Joseph, was obsessed with a certain animated train character. He refused to play with, or watch, anything else. Finally, a decision was made that the character needed to go "on holiday" (into the locked closet and not come out until some reinforcer sampling had been done).

The limiting of his access led to tantrums by Joseph. My colleagues and I were under strict obligation not to give into the tantrums by retrieving the toys and videos. The treatment plan in this case was a simple extinction plan, extinction being the term for when a behavior is not reinforced (in this case, not reinforcing the tantrums by giving Joseph the items).

Josephs' mom, Monica, however, was provided with a different set of rules than the staff. Monica was a single mother, working a great many hours and going to school to try to improve career options. She had little support. There were times when she just might not be able to successfully weather the tantrum and would give Joseph the toys/videos, just because she needed some peace. Her rule was, "When you put your key in the door, it's gut-check time." Basically, did she have the strength that night to carry out the plan, or did she not? If she felt strong enough, that was great. The toys/videos would stay in the closest. If that were not the case, however, if Monica was likely to give in to the tantrum, then *the very first time he asked for the items, she was to provide them.*

Was that preferable? Of course it was not. It would have been better if the things had stayed in the closet. At the very least, however, Monica was a "soda machine" (*continuous* reinforcement). Either tonight was a night when he could have the items, or tonight was a night when he could not have the items. Most crucially, Monica was never a "slot machine." Whatever Monica said *first* was the rule for the evening. She never changed her mind, particularly never giving in and giving the items after a long tantrum had occurred (*intermittent* reinforcement, only paying off every once in a while; see some of our other works for an extended discussion of the differential effects of continuous versus intermittent reinforcement). Joseph simply learned to "check in" with his mom. Whatever she said first was the rule for the night, he came to understand, and tantrums decreased and disappeared. Joseph learned to play with and watch other items.

As a final note on this matter, sometimes people who are asked to engage in such extinction procedures feel bad, as though they are being uncaring when they do not respond to the seeming or real upset of their child. If I may quote Avon, from the classic British science fiction series, *Blake's 7*, "I have never understood why it should be necessary to become irrational in order to prove that you care." Is it more caring to react emotionally and thereby reinforce the behavior and cause the inappropriate behavior to continue, or is it more caring to swallow one's own emotional reactions in the name of helping the person to overcome their behavioral deficit? I hope the answer is obvious.

Chapter Nineteen

"May I it's Raining Outside, Please": Addressing Speech Idiosyncrasies

It is unfortunately the case that many students diagnosed on the autism spectrum receive language instruction that is not what they need, either in intensity or in content. We can see a common example of this in students who go throughout their day making the American Sign Language (ASL) sign for "more." They don't have anything, but they want more of it. They have never been taught nouns or the structure of basic requesting, and staff and family are left puzzled. They know the student wants something, but the student has no way to communicate the specifics, and all are left playing guessing games.

The student that I will consider in the current chapter had the opposite difficulty. Staff working with him, particularly speech therapists, had made sure that he could make appropriate, full sentence requests. The problem was that this became the structure of all his communication, even declarative statements. Asked about the weather, he might reply, "May I it's raining outside, please."

Unfortunately, the student in question, named Daniel, had a history of very self-injurious behavior. Staff working with him were so glad to get the communication, and concerned about a return of the self-injurious behavior if they pushed for more typical communication, that they did not address his odd phrasing. Thus did his speaking style continue into adulthood, where I was introduced to him in an adult vocational placement. Daniel's vocational skills were such that he would easily be able to independently work within the store setting where he was learning his skills, but his language structure would greatly interfere with interactions with customers.

To address this, an intensive language instruction program was undertaken. As Daniel could read (although abstract comprehension was difficult) we chose to go with a scripting procedure, along with a careful shaping component. Basically, the grammatically correct answers to particular questions and comments would be written out for Daniel, and he would be encouraged to read these responses to staff when staff would strike up a conversation. Any responses that contained the extra words would lead to the interaction being repeated until Daniel was able to carry out the exchange without the extra words (i.e., "May I" and "please" when not appropriate to the sentence).

These scripts were practiced intensively, and the papers that contained the scripts were carefully faded over time. As Daniel mastered these scripted conversations, they were generalized to other settings, with staff members that Daniel did not know, but who had previously been coached regarding Daniel's language goals and expectations. When Daniel was successfully able to carry out these interactions, they were practiced with non-coached individuals and generalized to more spontaneous conversations. Through this intensive practice, the habit of adding the extra words had been eliminated from Daniel's language, except when appropriate.

Chapter Twenty

That's Not OK

I'm going to start this chapter by just coming out and saying it: It's not OK for boys to go the urinal and drop their pants and underwear around their knees or ankles. It's also not ok for them to establish sustained eye contact and start asking social questions, as we often teach people they are supposed to do when meeting others, while standing at the urinal.

Let me start with the latter issue. There is a basic rule in behavioral programming that you get what you program for – you don't get "what you meant to do." As I put it in another work, nature doesn't care what you intended. It only cares what actually happens.

Consider the following common eye contact drill:

Teacher: "Look at me."

(Student establishes eye contact to criteria)

Teacher: "That's good looking at me." (Turns away to take data)

Under these circumstances, what is it that you have taught the child? You have taught that:

1. Eye contact is something you make when someone specifically asks for it, and
2. As soon as the other person speaks, that means you're done and it's ok to look away.

Now, I'm sure that's not what you *meant* to teach, but it is the implicit message. Therefore, let me recommend an alternative:

Teacher: "Look at me."

(Student establishes eye contact to criteria)

Teacher: "That's good looking at me, point to crayon" (while holding up a crayon and a cup).

Notice the difference. In this latter case, we continue through a social interaction. The implicit message now is that eye contact is something you establish to begin a social interaction, and it continues until that social interaction is completed, not just until someone says something.

So it is with urinal etiquette. We often forget the social rules that have been established for particular settings, and that many individuals are extremely rule-governed in their behavior. I have learned a rule that I am supposed to interact with people I am meeting, showing social interest and striking up a conversation. What we often fail to program for is that such "rules" often have exceptions.

To illustrate what I mean regarding how adherence to rules can lead to difficulties, let me mention a student I was asked to observe at one time. I will encapsulate the issue in a script format:

Student: "Who do I sit with on the bus?"

Teacher: "Your friends."

Student: "Who are my friends?"

Teacher: "People who were in your class last year."

The next day on the bus, my student sits with someone who was in his class last year. That other student had nothing against my student, but that child wanted to sit with his sister as per his parental request and moves over to be with his sister. My student throws a tantrum on the bus:

"No, you're not doing it right! You're supposed to sit with your friends. We were in the same class last year, so we're friends so you're supposed to sit with me….!!!!"

As this example shows, the need to teach about such social situations, and quick and simple rules for social situations, without reference to context (such as the urinal) can lead to awkward social situations.

Let us return now to the dropping pants issue. There's just no way to put a nicer face on it. It simply isn't done. Not to be overly frightening about it, but you could not hold up a bigger sign that says "I have a social disability, please come and take advantage of me" than to have someone go to the urinal at the stadium or movie theater and drop pants and underwear below buttock-level.

This is one of those issues that is commonly dismissed as "we'll get to it later," and later never comes, or people don't even realize that it is an issue, as our 98% female staff begin to send older students into restrooms and do not monitor behavior within the bathroom. At first, everyone is just thrilled that the student is using the urinal appropriately, and doesn't sweat the small stuff. That minor detail, however, becomes huge as a socially stigmatizing behavior before all is said and done.

Please monitor such behavior and consider the social implications. If I may also provide a small hint, lots of guys don't even use the fly. First the pants are opened in the front (not lowered!). Then, for a right-handed young man, the left thumb hooks into the waistband of the underwear and pulls down slightly. The right hand takes the penis out over the top and aims towards the urinal (or towards the snow if spelling is involved).

Aren't you glad you read this chapter? Are you uncomfortable with my crude joke? Sorry, the student can't afford that. Your hesitancy to tackle a particular issue is impeding his social functioning. Please consider any other areas where this might be happening (e.g., Cristiane's chapter on teenage sexuality, to cite another commonly avoided area).

Chapter Twenty-One

Aggression, and an Argument for Home-based Crisis Intervention Training

Again, we're going to have to start this chapter somewhat bluntly. In my personal experience, physical aggression is the most commonly cited reason why supervised living arrangements outside the home are sought by parents for individuals diagnosed on the autism spectrum. This may take the form of physical aggression towards the parents themselves, towards other children or even infants in the home, or towards random individuals in the community.

We must first face a sobering reality. Children get bigger and stronger as they turn into adults, and parents and staff get older and weaker and slower (if we don't keep up on our training) over that same span. Aggression in a preschooler may be dismissed and, if you want to drive me mad, even called cute. When that same person is fifteen, trust me, it won't be cute anymore.

Another stark reality that we must face is the most basic of behavioral truths. Behavior that works (is reinforced) will continue to be displayed. If aggression, for example, leads to giving in to the student's demands or reducing requests made to the student, the aggression will become more likely. This, then, is the quintessential case of move with a purpose. Time is not on your side.

Let me draw a contrast. At a school where I was consulting, I was asked to step outside my caseload and help with a very young student who was being aggressive towards other students and throwing his body into dividing walls that were in the classroom to separate different activities (bouncing off the walls, literally!). When I entered the room, he had just thrown over a bucket of materials and was refusing to pick it up and was engaging in unsafe climbing on furniture. No time like the present; I verbally, and then physically, prompted him down from the furniture and directed him to a seat. He began to punch me in the chest, which I could easily extinguish (not showing the reinforcing reaction of verbally or physically engaging with him regarding the punching or removing my presence or my demands to sit and calm himself). After a relatively short period, he calmed and began to comply with my directions.

The teacher was horrified by what she had seen. When we later discussed it, she wondered aloud, "What if he had given you internal injuries?" I replied that I outweighed this student by more than one hundred pounds; he was not likely to damage me. She countered with, "Well, maybe you can handle it, but would you want your wife to be put at risk like that?" I didn't say it out loud, but that was a bad example. My wife routinely did this with students who outweighed her considerably. The central point is that I was looking to address this behavior while the student was still small enough that aggression could safely be extinguished. As my dear friend Nicole Rogerson put it at a conference: "We don't get bullied by people under four feet tall!"

Let me change gears, and talk about a student I worked with when he was nearly 20 years old. He weighed more than 300 pounds and could run the one hundred yard dash in under 10 seconds. He was strong, and he was fast. During one tantrum, as I was attempting to help him calm himself after he had aggressed towards a staff member, he had hit me sufficiently hard on the side of my head that I suffered a hearing loss.

As I always joke when discussing this, I have my obvious characteristics: I am short, I am balding, I am crude, I am highly opinionated. I bear a disturbing resemblance to Richard Dreyfuss in *Jaws*. I am not, however, suicidal. Writing extinction plans, and attempting to extinguish aggression in this student as I had done with the much younger student, would have been suicidal. Therefore, we used other treatment plans (functional communication training, Differential Reinforcement of Other behavior, redirection, etc.) to address aggression. It would be untrue, however, to say that we didn't also have to have formal crisis intervention procedures prepared.

Here we see our contrast. By the time we were facing the latter student's behavior, we were in a rough spot. We were in a position where if the student did engage in aggression, there was a strong chance of serious injury and crisis intervention procedures would have to be employed. Of course, we tried to create programming to avoid this (note, for example the work of Carr and Durand referenced by earlier authors), but we must admit we were working from a position that was less than ideal.

For students of all ages who may show aggressive behavior, it is my firm belief that there must be a plan. The Gentle Redirection of Aggressive and Destructive behavior (GRAD: Newman, 2011) program was created in order to satisfy an important need in the developmental disabilities field. Staff members working in facilities serving people with developmental disabilities are trained in crisis management and prevention (e.g., SCIP-R in New York). Similar trainings are provided to many individuals working in school settings through commercially available training packages. Yet, training for families of, and home-based caregivers for, individuals with developmental disabilities is not widely available.

That this should be the case flies in the face of much accepted clinical practice and logic. It is a basic statement of fact that families and home-based caregivers spend the majority of time with the individual with developmental disabilities. With this fact in mind, family and home-based caregiver training is recognized as crucial for maintaining behavioral, social, and linguistic gains. Family and home-based caregiver training in general behavioral and educational topics is thus provided as a matter of course, and no one questions the need for such training. Training stops being widely available, however, at the point of crisis management training, with regrettable results. To be blunt, as noted at the outset of this chapter, the ability of families and home-based caregivers to prevent and manage physical crises often means the difference between an individual with a developmental disability being able to continue living in a home setting and having to move into a more restrictive environment such as a group home or residence.

The absence of crisis prevention and management programs for families and home-based caregivers has two possible causes:

1. A belief that it is not needed, that the training in general behavior management and general educational principles alluded to above is sufficient.
2. A fear of misuse of procedures and consequent injuries to family members or to the individual with the developmental disability.

The first objection can be easily dismissed. If that training in general behavioral and educational concepts truly was sufficient, why would additional crisis intervention and prevention training be needed for staff members in schools and other facilities? Obviously, if staff members working in such facilities require additional training to prevent and to manage crises, then families and caregivers require the same training. I'm not going to lie about it. As mentioned above, I have been physically hurt, including dislocations and a hearing loss, in having to perform crisis intervention over the past two plus decades. If that has happened to me after receiving training, not to mention decades of competitive athletics, do we imagine that things are perfectly safe for those who are not given training?

The second objection is a bit more difficult to answer. It is true that the schools and other facilities serving individuals with developmental disabilities often provide a greater level of supervision and structure, not to mention sheer numbers of persons available, than a typical home setting. For that reason, it is considered safer to provide training in crisis prevention and management in the facilities, as the greater amount of structure and supervision and person-power would help to prevent abuses and accidents.

Even allowing for the possible truth of this argument, however, one has to ask, "Then what?" We are still left with the basic truth mentioned above. It is the family and home-based caregivers who are going to spend the majority of time with the individual with the developmental disability. If we accept that there may be physical crises, then what are the families and home-based caregivers supposed to do? Without training, they are left to:

1. "Do the best they can" (which may lead to injuries to self or to the individual or to potentially dangerous object-destructive behavior).
2. Call the police (which may lead to unneeded hospitalizations).
3. Walk on eggshells around the individual for fear of creating a crisis situation (which may lead to long-term behavioral regression as the individual has aggressive and destructive behavior reinforced or is simply never pushed to improve skills for fear of creating a crisis).
4. Pursue drug treatments that may lead to serious and undesirable side-effects.

Clearly, each of these options has unacceptable pitfalls associated with it. Training to more efficiently handle crises is therefore crucial for everyone, families and home-based caregivers included. We have to remember our basic bottom line: behavior that works is kept. If aggression leads to reduced demands of the student, or giving in to their demands, it will maintain and possibly escalate. At some point in the not too distant future, then, we will be in a rather unpleasant discussion regarding what is *possible* in terms of addressing the behavior, not what is most desirable.

As a final note on this, I wish to just be very clear on the difference between crisis intervention and behavior treatment plans. Briefly stated, do you have to perform crisis management interventions very frequently? If you do, then you are not really doing crisis management, you are doing behavior treatment interventions (and probably not as efficiently as possible, because if it was going well, you wouldn't be having frequent crisis-level flare-ups). Crises should be fairly infrequent. If such behavior is occurring frequently, then we are out of the realm of crisis management and are really into the realm of behavior management and behavior treatment plans and we will need to conduct Functional Behavior Assessments/Analyses to determine what may be maintaining the behavior and therefore how to design a proper treatment plan.

Chapter Twenty-Two

Reducing a Behavior that Sucks

Sibel Tenish

"He finds the dummy comforting," the parents tell me at the autism early intervention clinic where I work in Sydney. "It calms him down," they say. Yes of course it does, because a pacifier (or a 'dummy' as we Australians like to call it) provides a form oral stimulation to the child. It likely serves as a positive reinforcer for the child. No doubt, the pacifier also serves as a negative reinforcer for the parents: child cries and parent gets a headache, child stops crying when sucking on a dummy and headache disappears. It is no wonder that we see so many three year olds walking around with a silicone teat in their mouths!

While a pacifier may have some benefits, it certainly has its risks as well. The overuse of a pacifier has been associated with a higher risk of ear infections, dental problems such as cavities, protruding or crooked teeth, and delayed speech. This is why it is often recommended that parents start to wean their children off pacifiers when they are about 10 months old.

Some of the most common features of autism include significant delays in speech, lack of social skills, and the presentation of stereotypic behaviors. In view of these difficulties, I suggest that it is especially important for a child with autism to be 'weaned off' the pacifier sooner rather than later. Certainly, no one would want to risk delaying their child's speech even further, or allowing them to look socially inappropriate around their peers, by letting them walk around with a large dummy in their mouth at the age of four. The question therefore becomes, "How do I wean my child off that dummy?" I like to refer to the three Cs: Competition, Choice, and Consistency. These three rules can be used with any child, regardless of well-developed or lagging skills. Please allow me to demonstrate how these rules were applied through the presentation of a case study, my nephew.

At the beginning of last summer (remember I live in Australia, so I'm referring to December 2010), my sister expressed that she wanted to start weaning my nephew off the dummy. My nephew, who I nicknamed Little Bob when he started wearing a yellow helmet and showed great pleasure in watching all things Bob the Builder, was due to have his 2nd birthday in January 2011, but was still, as my sister put it, "Hooked on the dummy!" Little Bob's interest in the dummy was not just a phase, as Bob the Builder turned out to be. It seemed like an addiction. I say this because as soon as my nephew was done with his meal, he would demand his dummy. If he wasn't eating or talking, he was sucking on that thing to his heart's content, like many smokers I know!

When Little Bob wasn't given his dummy, he'd start to cry. When he started to cry, his parents gave him his dummy to stop him from crying. Naturally, Little Bob learned that when he cried, his crying would be reinforced with the dummy. As evidence of this, we saw that his crying behavior shortly after a meal was on the rise. It took my husband and I two weekends to teach Little Bob that having a dummy in his mouth 24/7 was not very cool, and he wouldn't be allowed to use his dummy when he was at our house. The advantage that my husband David and I had was that we had a few highly preferred toys and activities, which the visiting kids were only able to access when they were at our house. Among these super-special reinforcers were a particular Bob the Builder toy set, a favorite Bob the Builder DVD, and a swimming pool to cool us off on those very hot days. We knew that each of these could compete with the dummy, as when we offered a choice, Little Bob chose both nearly equally. So, we gave him two choices: he could have access to one of the competing activities but would have to put his dummy away or, he could keep sucking his dummy while David, myself, and Little Bob's sister enjoyed the activities ourselves. We also paired these activities with a lot of positive attention, praising and high- fiving Little Bob's sister for not having a dummy, so she became a great role model. It wasn't long before Little Bob decided to put the dummy in his pocket and join us. The activities that were initially competing against the dummy became reinforcing enough to increase the desired outcome, dummy out of mouth. Any time that my nephew wanted to put the dummy back in his mouth, he was presented with the 2 choices again and if he chose the dummy, he was denied access to the previously established reinforcer. The advantage of having a few reinforcers at hand to choose from was that if satiation occurred (if he no longer desired one of them), there were at least 2 other activities to offer.

Fortunately, the following weekend was another hot one so we invited my sisters over to our house, which gave us the opportunity to practice those rules again: dummy out of mouth equaled access to reinforcers. We were consistent in our approach time after time and, eventually, my nephew learned that no dummies were allowed at our place. He even started to give his dummy to his mum, voluntarily, as they walked up the steps leading to our front door. The constant pairing of ourselves with reinforcers and the consistency in our approach meant that we no longer had to find things that would compete with the dummy. Little Bob continued to whinge and cry for his dummy at home and at daycare, but when David and I were around, he immediately announced that he was putting his dummy in a safe place.

I should note that, initially, David and I did allow my nephew to have his dummy in one condition, when he was going to sleep. We were quite specific with this condition too: pajamas were worn and games were over. It was quiet time and Little Bob had to lie down. I wanted to mention this to illustrate that it doesn't have to be "all or nothing." For some parents, the thought of going cold turkey and having to cope with their child's challenging behaviors late at night is scary. The key is consistency.

Once we saw success, it was time to generalize Little Bob's success to his home. We made sure everyone followed the rules: establish reinforcers, present the choices, and stick with it. When you're ready to increase your expectations, you can apply the same 3 rules and hopefully, get rid of that silicone teat sooner rather than later!

Chapter Twenty-Three

The Not So Happy 4th of July

David M. Newman

(Bobby's note: I asked David to put the experience from chapter one into the form of a skit that elementary school children could read at their level and perform to explore concepts in behavior. You can feel free to replicate his example with stories from this book and *Behavioral Detectives* and other such media. By acting out the scenarios, students will achieve a better understanding of the behavioral principals involved. Feel free to copy this chapter, we promise not to sue. Feel free to have graduate students act also.)

(Opening scene: Charles and his Dad are walking to a refreshment stand on the beach, having just finished a round of body-surfing. They are a bit wet and tired, but happy.)

CHARLES

What a perfect day for the 4th of July! Hey, why don't we get something to eat?

DAD

Sure.

(Charles and Dad go to the refreshment stand. Charles goes and finds a table and sits down. Dad waits on line. Kids jump around and scream and carry on. Dawn and Daniela are at counter.)

OWEN

Hey, Rebecca!!! Watch me!

(Owen jumps off of the table.)

REBECCA

No way. That's too easy!

OWEN

Then prove it!

REBECCA

No!

JADA

Get off of my hand, Dylan!

(Charles sits there with his mouth wide open.)

DYLAN

NO! I want to do a backflip.

JADA

But Dylan, you could kill yourself!

DAWN (in distance at counter)

That's why I love that show!

(Daniela and Dawn laugh.)

DANIELA

Oh, excuse me for one moment. KIDS!!! If you don't stop now, you are not getting your ice cream!!

OWEN

What??? No SpongeBob bars!?!?!

DAD (to himself)

Yeah, like that would ever happen . . .

(Other kids continue yelling and jumping off furniture, adults ignore them.)

DAWN

OMG! Daniela did you read about . . . ? (voice fades)

(Dad drops his mouth open. Jada walks over to Charles.)

JADA

Hi, my name is Jada.

CHARLES

Hi, my name is Charles. I've seen you at school.

JADA

I have some pretty freaky brothers and sisters, as you can see.

CHARLES

Yeah. Do you want to eat with us?

JADA

Would I ever!

DAD

OK! The food is ready. Plus, I got some extra.

CHARLES

This is my new friend, Jada. She goes to my school.

DAD

Hi, Jada.

CHARLES/JADA

We want to eat together!

DAD

Do you want to eat here or by the towels?

CHARLES/JADA

By the towels!

DAD

Are you sure that's OK with your mom?

(Jada looks at Daniela and Dawn.)

JADA

I'm sure she'll be fine with it, but I'll ask her. She saw you two bodysurfing and said she knows you from school events. Anyway, our towels are really close to yours and they can see me from here and there.

(Jada quickly talks to the two ladies, then points to where they will be. Charles, Jada, and Dad exit.)

THE END

There were some right things and wrong things in this play. The right things were Charles inviting Jada to be his friend, seeing that she was not happy sitting with the wild behavior of her siblings. It was also good that Jada wasn't jumping around.

Here are some of the bad things: the kids shouldn't have been jumping around like wild monkeys! The parents shouldn't have threatened them with "NO ICE CREAM!" if that wasn't ever going to happen ("don't say it if you aren't going to do it!"). The adults might have also complimented Jada on not acting so wildly ("catch 'em being good!").

Also on the bad side, Jada shouldn't have walked away from her family, no matter how jerky they were acting. That Charles and his dad were familiar doesn't make it safe. You should talk about all of this with the class.

Here are some helpful tips if you are going to put on this play.

SCENE

This is a hot summer beach day on the 4th of July. You may want to have some sand by the refreshment stand. You will need a table and make sure you have a soft ground for the kids to land in while they are jumping.

PROPS

You will need fake food and chairs to and a counter to make a refreshment stand.

CHARACTERS

In order of appearance:

Charles

Dad

Owen

Rebecca

Jada

Dylan

Dawn

Daniela

COSTUMES

Everyone can wear generally anything, as long as it seems beachy.

This is supposed to be a fun show to do, so everyone should have fun. At the end of the show, if you are performing it for an audience, take a minute at the end before everyone takes their bows, and ask the audience the rights and wrongs of the characters in the show. Be prepared to ask questions to give them ideas, if necessary.

Chapter Twenty-Four
Why Does Ollie Play with Trains for Hours on End Without Getting Bored?

Cassie le Fevre

Ollie (name completely fictitious because we liked the way it sounded) was three years old and lived at home with his parents and older sister. His parents were at their wits' end. Even at such a young age, he was fascinated with trains. He would watch his electric train for hours, going round and round the track. If the trains were packed away he would cry, scream and throw himself on the floor. The crying would last an eternity, and if it stopped it was replaced by a repetitive sequence – Ollie would follow the same path around the house with his head bowed and make high-pitched noises. It was too much for his parents; they would bring the trains back out and allow Ollie to play with them as much as he wanted. The trains became the lesser of two evils. Unfortunately it meant that Ollie didn't do much else and the longer he watched the trains, the more upset he became when he was required to leave them – such as when the family needed to leave the house, or eat dinner or go to sleep.

It's one of those chicken and egg scenarios. Is the child engaging in repetitive behaviors too frequently and therefore doesn't develop any alternate leisure skills, or are they bored, don't know what else to do and engage in repetitive behaviors? One of the first questions I ask a family is, "What does your child like to do to amuse himself? What is he interested in?" It was clear that Ollie did not have any independent play skills and had not yet found pleasure in alternative activities. Trains are fun. They have small moving parts and are predictable, but it wasn't to say that Ollie wouldn't also find figurine play enjoyable or reading a book or building with Lego. When encouraged to play with different toys or engage in functional activities, Ollie refused, lay down and closed his eyes until he was able to go right back to his trains, demonstrating no interest in the wonderfully varied and stimulating toys his parents tried to introduce. What we needed to find was the motivation to encourage Ollie to try these alternative activities.

The simplest option would have been to merely remove the trains, put up with the tantrum and hope that Ollie would eventually "get over it." I'm sure he would have stopped crying eventually. The concern was, what would Ollie do instead to occupy his time? He had no other independent play skills and wasn't interested in other toys or activities. There was a real risk that the replacement behavior would be more inappropriate and potentially dangerous. His history indicated that Ollie's alternative behavior was to walk around the house making ear-piercing noises and nobody in the household enjoyed experiencing that.

Instead, Ollie's family members were taught to carefully and systematically increase his exposure to alternate activities whilst still being able to watch his trains. We knew several things about Ollie:

1. He had very limited language but could understand simple instructions and request common foods and objects and
2. He loved M&Ms almost as much as he loved trains.

So the first thing we did was hide the M&Ms for two weeks. Deprivation is a powerful thing, and if Ollie hadn't eaten any of his favorite treats for a long while they were potentially going to be a powerful reinforcer. We then sat down and brainstormed potential activities that Ollie might come to enjoy. The group, which included his older sister Lucy, decided that it might be beneficial to not deviate too far from the train theme. His parents collected a pile of toys, including some exciting looking trucks and cars, a 9-piece train inset puzzle, a toy garage with working parts and a simple electronic game where if you touched a train it would follow a path along a train track.

The next step was slightly more difficult; Ollie's family was aware that the process was possibly going to be slow and tedious. We firstly allowed Ollie to watch his trains as we placed one of the new toys close to the train track. If Ollie tolerated the presence of the toy, we gave him lots of praise and an M&M and moved the toy closer. Eventually, we were able to place the toy next to the train as it moved around the track. From there we would stop the train moving round the track momentarily, show Ollie the new toy (e.g., a toy car) and the second he looked at it we praised him, gave him an M&M, and allowed the train to continue around the track. We moved from showing Ollie the toy to asking him to touch it, then to hold it for increasing periods of time, and then to imitate another person playing with the toy (pushing it along the ground, for example), reinforcing every step of the way. Within a few weeks, Ollie was happily imitating the play of a family member for five minutes before going back to his beloved trains. The M&Ms were faded out, and his family would generally use praise to reinforce trying new activities.

Time passed and the intervention continued. Ollie began to understand the concept of "First . . . then . . ." with the use of a visual schedule. This helped his parents to be able to tell Ollie that first he would be playing with a puzzle or electronic game and *then* he could watch his trains. He was introduced to a variety of activities and was starting to play independently with each for brief periods of time. His sister was an eager role model and would demonstrate new play sequences for Ollie to copy, delighted when he could do what she did. The most exciting day for the family came when Ollie's mother woke up one morning to find that Ollie had gotten himself out of bed and chosen to play with a pair of dump trucks and some Lego blocks instead of going straight to his trains.

Ollie is now five and, if you look carefully, you can still see the train set sitting in the corner of his bedroom. You can also see elaborate Lego constructions, a football, figurines from various movies, a car racing track and several Transformers scattered around his room. He still enjoys playing with his sister, although their tastes are now quite different. The most pleasing news for his parents is that he no longer spends hours at a time watching trains or walking in circuits around the house. Ollie has functional, independent play skills and can find generally find something to do to occupy his time. He has also learned to come to his parents and tell them he is bored, something that most typical children will do but something that parents often find completely frustrating. We developed another intervention to reduce this behavior too . . . but that's a whole other story!

Chapter Twenty-Five

Toilet Training and Consistency

Ana C. Madeira

Research shows that potty training is not an easy task for children diagnosed on the autism spectrum. Parents with children diagnosed with ASDs have noted that potty training can be frustrating for them, often questioning their child's readiness. Often, if the child is a boy, parents may use the excuse that boys are lazy. When I hear parents mentioning such reasons, I think to myself that if a child is healthy they can be potty trained. It might take longer for one child to get potty trained then another, but that's okay. Then I just have to convince the parents.

Gawley, Stephenson, Roane, Bouxsein, and Veenstra (2011) discuss teaching a child with an ASD how to self-monitor and initiate use of the bathroom. They used a watch that functioned as a discriminative stimulus for toileting initiations, teaching the student to approach the target therapist and sign "bathroom." The alarm served as an auditory stimulus and it was effective at promoting acquisition of independent initiation for toileting. Smith, Smith, and Lee (2000) discuss how to work with the child who has become used to eliminating in the diaper and has difficulty transferring to the toilet.

Shabani, Katz, Wilder, Beauchamp, Taylor, and Fischer (2002) describe how the use of prompts has been shown to effectively increase social initiations in children who rarely initiated spontaneously. The purpose of this study was to conduct a systematic replication of Smith, et al. to teach a child with an ASD to decrease the use of diapers, thereby gradually increasing the use of the toilet at home.

Adem is a 5-year-old boy who was diagnosed with autism. He is enrolled in a self-contained class in a public school near his home. The parents communicated to me, as his new therapist, that toileting was a very difficult skill to teach Adem at home. They also informed me that Adem was using the toilet at school but had not generalized the target to their home. Adem was put in diapers when he traveled to and from school, and he would not use the toilet with his parents. He would engage in aggressive behaviors such as kicking, throwing himself on the floor, and running away from his parents when they tried to bring him to the bathroom. Adem's parents were very frustrated with his being so adamant against using the toilet at home.

After getting Adem's background information, I sat with the parents and discussed what the next step would be. I asked the parents to take data on the times that Adem had a wet or dry diaper, as well as what he ate and drank and the time. This was important so that we could know when he might need to go to the bathroom and what might make Adem go to the bathroom more rapidly. I asked that data be collected for two weeks.

After Adem's parents collected the data, I looked it over for any patterns that might appear. I sat with Adem's parents and discussed the techniques that were to be used with Adem. The first step was to take the diapers away. Adem used the toilet at school and that needed to be carried over to home. Removing the diaper during travel was also important: NO DIAPERS AT ALL. We then began a bathroom routine with Adem. His parents made a schedule of when Adem needed to be taken to the bathroom. The last step was having a strong reinforcer for Adem when he was dry and also when he successfully eliminated in the toilet.

Starting toilet training at home did not affect the behavior at school. The first week of the toilet training was very hard on his parents, and also on Adem. He was having accidents and he ran away when he was wet and cried when he was taken to the bathroom.

As mentioned, the first step of toilet training was the removal of diapers from the home. His parents told Adem that he was a big boy and that he needed to use underwear. Adem resisted at first, but after a few tries he accepted the underwear. Whenever Adem appropriately put on his underwear, walked to the bathroom, or sat on the toilet, verbal praise was given. Once the timer was put into place, Adem had to go to the bathroom every 30 minutes. Adem was very defiant at first, but after he realized that he would have time on the iPod for appropriate going to the bathroom, his behavior changed. Adem would sit on the toilet for about 10 minutes, or until he had a successful elimination. The adult present at that time would immediately reinforce this with verbal praise and the iPod.

Adem's accidents decreased and his successes increased with his therapist, babysitter, and dad. He remained defiant when his mother was alone at home. Adem's mother had a hard time hearing him cry and asking to be taken off the toilet. Adem's mother was advised that she had to be strong and not give in. I started staying later to support Adem's mother and help her to be strong and follow through. Adem just needed to see his mother follow through one time, and he was actually very upset when that happened. After a few minutes of his mother not giving in and instead reminding Adem that he needed to eliminate in the toilet, he finally went and his mother gave him verbal praise and the iPod right away.

Once the routine was consistent and everyone followed the procedure, Adem was toilet trained. Adem's parents were very excited and they couldn't believe how fast Adem was trained. Adem's mother always said, "I thought it was going to take a year for him to use the toilet."

In closing, toilet training Adem has made him more independent in his everyday routines. Adem just needed the adults around him to be more consistent and needed strong reinforcers for this behavior. As of writing, we are working on having Adem learn to initiate going to the bathroom.

Chapter Twenty-Six

Shop Till You Drop (Dead)

Nicole Rogerson

"I would rather be at home with a pencil in my eye."

That was my feeling every time I had to take my autistic son to a supermarket or shopping mall. I mean really; why would I want to take him to a loud, crowded noisy place full of things he wanted so he could tantrum, grab, abscond and scream? Why risk it? Why put yourself through the trauma and humiliation of your fellow shoppers judging you as World's Worst Parent? Why, when you don't have to? It is a digital age, buy it all online. Forget the stares, the tantrums, the gut-wrenching pain and sadness that only a parent of a child diagnosed on the autism spectrum would recognize. Just get in online and move on!

This is the diatribe I gave my son's Program Supervisor after a particularly eventful Sunday afternoon grocery shopping at our local mall. We live in the city, so shopping centers are full on the weekend, filled with busy working people who "forgot to have children" (zero tolerance of tantrums) or "professional parents" who were too busy to shop during the week, as they were ferrying their child between advanced violin lessons and toddler Latin extension classes.

So, as my son clearly can't go to a shopping center, I will bring the shopping center to him. I mean why not do it all online? That is when my Program Supervisor chimed in with the obvious point that, whilst my son couldn't currently manage supermarket shopping, it didn't mean he never would. We apparently could teach him the skills to do this and therefore give him an independent living skill for the rest of his life. Well, all right, if you put it that way.

I have never met a behavior that wasn't better managed with a behavior plan. We needed a set of clear guidelines, procedures, and criteria for mastery before moving to the next level. To engage in some foreshadowing, the first and most important thing to remember before undertaking this effort is to remember to NEVER PRACTICE THIS WHEN YOU ACTUALLY NEED FOOD! This is a behavior management plan, not simply tips for what might work in this situation. You need to treat this plan like you would any other. Break the task into small achievable steps, practice, practice, practice, and always reinforce.

So our shopping plan started on a Tuesday morning at 10 a.m. in a suburban grocery store. Why 10 a.m.? That's simple: the morning commuters have been through, and it is too early for school mums planning dinner. Grocery stores are quiet at 10 a.m., mid-week. They are often too quiet, so it is a perfect time to practice without the added stress of crowds. To prepare, we wrote a note, including 3 very clear pictures of things we were going to buy from the store. I would recommend choosing 3 things that are easy to find, that your child knows and loves, and that are never out of stock. So, the plan is for junior to walk into the store, holding my hand to get three things. It probably goes without saying, but walk fast! Get this thing over and done with quickly, so a problem behavior doesn't have time to rear its head. All the time he was walking next to me I was praising him for being so good.

We raced in, grabbed the 3 items and then bolted for the checkout. Cash, people! Let's not complicate things with cards. In, out, pay cash, freddo frog as a reinforcer (a chocolate freddo was my son's reinforcer of choice, if you can find something that will be just as reinforcing which is healthier and not a food treat – then good for you). I might also add that for some children your first trip may have to just be in and out with no purchasing at all. We need to start where the child is. Can he even tolerate entering the store, let alone shopping?

So, was my son miraculously better in supermarkets or did we just do that so fast he didn't get the chance to be anything but? Well of course it was the latter, but it was a start. The next time we practiced this was not in a week's time. It was within a day. We did the same thing: 3 items, paying cash, at 10 in the morning. Jack was learning that shopping wasn't always a long drawn-out affair, he was practicing "good holding hands," and getting a treat for doing so. We were getting a lot of success; it was time to up the ante. Let's buy 6 things at 10 a.m. with cash. No problem at all . . . okay, let's use a credit card (EFTPOS here Down Under).

Once all of these individual steps were mastered and Jack was having a lot of practice in behaving appropriately at the supermarket, it was again time to go to the next level. How quickly you can move through steps is individualized, of course. Some children need very gradual build-up. Jack was being so successful, though, that we decided it was time for the 3:30 p.m. shop. This is, of course, the most evil time of the day. School is out, kids are everywhere and mums are trawling the aisles looking for inspiration for dinner. We decided to go back a step to 3 things and cash if we were going to tackle the busier time slot. The strategy was familiar: in and out, fast and successful, allowing for lots of opportunities for reinforcement.

The key was practice, setting achievable steps, moving through the stages and making it fun. Even I was starting to like it!

So what was mastery? I used to say it was a full trolley, Saturday afternoon, and a credit card which was being declined. All these years later, however, it is handing him $50 and a list and he goes shopping for me!

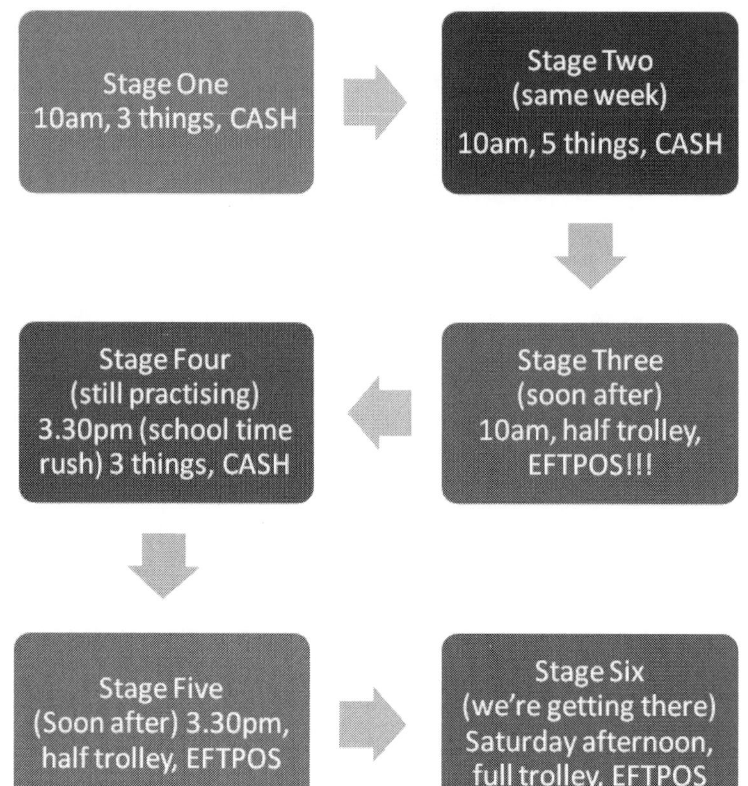
Stage One
10am, 3 things, CASH
Stage Two
(same week)
10am, 5 things, CASH
Stage Three
(soon after)
10am, half trolley,
EFTPOS!!!
Stage Four
(still practising)
3.30pm (school time
rush) 3 things, CASH
Stage Five
(Soon after) 3.30pm,
half trolley, EFTPOS
Stage Six
(we're getting there)
Saturday afternoon,
full trolley, EFTPOS

Chapter Twenty-Seven

My Brother Joey

Lillianna Rogers

My name is Lillianna Rogers. I go by Lily for short. I am twelve. I have two brothers. Joey is ten and has autism. Matthew is nine and doesn't have autism. When Joey was little, he cried all day. He pinched people, he hit people, he cried at night, he ran around in circles, he wouldn't eat food, he took his clothes off, he ate things that weren't food, he broke my toys, he scribbled on anything he could find, he made it hard for us to go anywhere but home, and I couldn't have friends over. There was so much to work on that we didn't know which thing to pick. Mom and Dad would make lists and talk it over with professionals. They would ask me and Matthew questions to see what bothered our lives the most. Mom tried to work on anything that hurt us most like the pinching, or the things that kept us from having friends over like the taking his clothes off. But what I wanted was for her to work on the things that made Joey the saddest.

When I was little and Joey would cry a lot, it seemed simple for me. I thought Joey was crying because he was sad. Mom would say he is trying to communicate, but I didn't believe her because he just looked upset to me. So we e-mailed Bobby Newman together. Mom always asked him questions and she told me I could any time as well. So I told Bobby how Joey cried all the time and I asked Bobby why Joey was sad. I thought he was sick or not feeling well. Bobby told me the reasons Joey might be crying. There were lots of reasons! It wasn't always because he was sad or not feeling well. I felt better because Bobby was a doctor, so I believed him. Since then, I always just ask a question that is on my mind. I tell everyone who has a brother or sister with autism to ask questions. I wish we told more kids to do that. Joey is ten now and because of all of my questions I can do things that are easy and that help Joey. I understand things I wouldn't about him if I hadn't asked the questions.

When we go places, even places just for kids with autism, I think there are lots of kids with autism but some have a harder time than others. I think Joey has a lot of things to work on all of the time, and it is not fair because most other kids with autism that I meet don't have this much to work on. I get sad about this, but it doesn't last long because I am confident that we can do something about it. If I didn't understand this, if I didn't see how hard work could change something, I would be sad all the time. I think we should share information with kids with this purpose in mind. Kids can be a lot of help, if they know what to do. There are many things I do for Joey.

When Joey is outside and running in circles, I follow him and play chase. I make this behavior into something I think other kids do so he won't get made of fun of. When Joey repeats something over and over, I ask my Mom or his teachers questions about why he does that. I use their answers to help Joey. I learned that Joey likes when people say things with a lot of emotion. So, if I want to teach him a new phrase I say it in the funniest way I can so he will remember it the fastest. Some of my favorite phrases that Joey says are, "I love Lily," and "Have a good day." He mimics Grandma and says, "Oh my God!" I'm trying to teach him, "Oh my gosh!" I make the shhh sound really strongly so he hears it best. When Joey says phrases that I think other kids will laugh at, I tell my parents other things that kids our age say instead.

When Joey walks up the stairs, he walks up two stairs and down one and then back up two stairs. I thought we could teach him to count the stairs because he doesn't like to repeat any numbers so he might not want to walk down a stair he already counted. I know what kind of pants Joey feels comfortable in. I tell my parents what ones he likes that he will get made fun of for wearing. Sometimes we still let him wear them but it is a good thing for my parents to know.

Mom and Dad have videotaped me and Matthew playing games or doing activities that we want Joey to learn because he learns best with videos. In fact, he watches them over and over again! We try to use this to our advantage. When Joey was eating pencils, me and Matthew went to school and watched for any kids that were chewing on something other than food or gum (Joey doesn't like gum). We saw kids who kept straws from lunch in their mouth all day. So we taught Joey to chew on a juice box straw. He does this all the time at school and no one laughs at him. Just today, Joey was making loud noises and laughing. I sat next to him and mimicked his noises but made them sound more like singing. Each time he makes this noise I will sit next to him and sing until he slowly changes what his noise sounds like.

We aren't perfect. When we were working on the pencil problem, we were supposed to keep the pencils out of sight. I forgot all the time. Mom taped a half eaten pencil to the fridge to "help me remember." It was funny. Joey can only be naked in his bedroom. Mom fired the person who broke this rule. That is funny too. We call it the naked room (not when my friends are around though, and they can come over now). Joey covered our toilet seat with my nail polish. We left it like that because it was prettier that way and made us laugh every time we looked at it. My friends asked me what exploded in our toilet. I said it was a nail polish bomb. There are many funny things to talk about.

There are a lot of things I can do for Joey and I feel better being able to do them. But I can only do them if I can ask questions and learn. I am grateful that my parents let me ask my own questions directly to Bobby from the time I was little because now I can feel helpful instead of sad. When my mom gets upset about how this life affects my brother Matthew and I, I can tell her to stop trying to make our lives average because we will never live an average life. But we live a happy life. We live a great life together as a family. Joey would still be doing all the things he used to if it weren't for us. But it isn't just my Mom and Dad who get to feel good about it. We all feel pride for ourselves and we are proud of Joey.

Joey inspires me to do things I wouldn't normally do, like stand up for kids who are being bullied. He has taught me to be true to myself. I try to be exactly who God made me to be. I want Joey to be exactly who God made him to be, too. I like being able to help him and I like the funny things he does. I think it is funny that he carved a 3 on his pumpkin instead of a face. I try to teach him how to do the things he likes to do without getting made fun of. He wants to have friends so badly. He cries when he comes home from school when he gets made fun of, or the teachers talked about him. People think he can't hear because he doesn't talk all the time. So I try to teach him how to do all the things that make him happy without getting picked on. I am his sister and closest to his age, so I think I am the best person to do this. Plus I love him.

Chapter Twenty-Eight

To Let Be or To Not Let Be: THAT is the Question

Jennica Nill

Recently I was reminded that the range of knowledge and misconceptions for families of children with autism is as broad as the spectrum itself. My husband and I took our three children to a play in New York City. It was a special event for families of children with disabilities. One of our children has autism. His behavior was excellent during the entire show, to which another parent commented, "You are so lucky that your child has the capabilities to act appropriately in public, many children with autism can't act the way society expects them to act." The last part of the statement wasn't what bothered me most; it was the "lucky" part. Luck has had nothing to do with it!

Our second oldest son was diagnosed with autism in early 2001. Once we began his intervention program, I began reading everything I could get my hands on to learn more about autism and the expected prognosis. What fueled me most was finding stories in books and on the internet written by parents that included what their child's functioning level was at diagnosis and then fast forwarded a few months or even years of intervention, to how they were functioning now. Wide eyed and heart racing, I would compare what was described with how my son was responding. Story after story, it became very clear there was a correlation between the rate at which your child gains skills and the likelihood of overcoming the behavioral excesses and deficits that define autistic spectrum disorder.

The first two years after diagnosis, I was in a bit of a hokey pokey. I had one foot in and one foot out of this new autism world that I previously knew little about. I wasn't totally in denial; I will admit, however, that I told myself, "We'll be out of this by the time he's three." In hindsight, I did know that it might not happen and was completely aware that his responding was slow and steady. His deficits were significant, his excesses pervasive. When left to his own devices, he spent his time "practicing his autism" in the form of odd repetitive movements, wandering aimlessly, fast forwarding and rewinding VHS tapes, making frequent noises and flapping his hands. He would get upset if I didn't drive the same way to school every day, or if I drove past McDonalds without stopping. He had limited verbal ability, which would contribute to his behavioral outbursts. As with many children with autism, other diagnoses followed, what professionals call "co-morbid" conditions. These included anxiety disorder, apraxia of speech, and cognitive disability.

Everywhere we went was challenging. When the kids were around 3 and 4 years old, we were at a local zoo. Dustin's older brother, Jake, was excited to see the puppet show. We took a seat and, within a few minutes, it became clear that we couldn't stay. Dustin's vocalizations, rocking, and protesting to get up were too disruptive to everyone around us. We had to leave, at which point Jake started sobbing, "Mom, Dustin ruins everything!" Although I would always try to go places with my boys, it was easier to just stay home. Even in the most embracing of environments, like local events only for families of children with autism, I would find myself bringing Dustin outside and hanging out in the minivan while he tantrumed to leave. While I know that autism-friendly events are specifically meant for families like mine, and so we do not have to worry if he acts out at the movies or other public venues, I felt it was not fair to the other children with autism and their siblings that my son's tantruming in the form of screaming, yelling, and falling to the floor would get *them* upset and trigger *their* behaviors. At almost age 4, Dustin was still drinking from a bottle and was not toilet trained. Although he was learning language and gaining skills, the stress caused by his behavioral deficits was taking a toll on the family. This could not be the way, could it? Do I just let him be? Is he so affected by his disability that this is just how it is and I need to accept it? He was getting special services, and even they told me that I had to accept he would plateau. I was feeling helpless and hopeless.

It was then that I began to connect on-line with families and started to go to conferences presented by experts in the field of ABA. I did not know there were actually behavior specialists known as Board Certified Behavior Analysts that you could hire for evaluations and to make recommendations. It was at this time that I received the most important advice I ever received. I was told that I needed to take my son anywhere and everywhere as much as possible. I should not leave him at home with others while I ran out to the store because it is easier; it would only get harder as he got older if I didn't address it now. He needed to learn to adapt and needed constant exposure for that opportunity, and I needed to learn how to teach it. The longer I waited, the more likely that I would no longer be able to bring him anywhere. The reality of our situation hit me hard. If my son never learned how to act appropriately, never learned that there are other ways to express himself and control his behaviors, or was not consistently held to behavioral expectations, I was not helping him; his and our family's quality of life would continue to deteriorate. He would be publicly perceived as more impaired than he truly is. He would not be treated with the dignity and respect he deserves for his different abilities. He would not get the opportunity to live a full and meaningful, happy life. There was also the realization that I would not live forever to protect him.

Through our consultants and conferences, I learned how and when to address his behaviors. I learned that all of these behaviors Dustin was engaging in were not just because he has autism, they were serving a purpose for him. They were actually a form of communication that could be changed and replaced with more appropriate and socially acceptable behaviors. I learned how to shape his behaviors, when to ignore, and when to give attention. I learned that a reinforcer is not something I thought he would like, but something that I know increases the probability of a behavior, and I learned how to use them proactively. I followed the advice and took him anywhere and everywhere, even places that I didn't need to go. I gained confidence in my parenting ability and quickly saw improvements. Knowing what to do and how to do it is key, because if you accidently handle behaviors and reinforcement in the wrong way, or if you and those directly involved in your child's life are inconsistent, you can actually make the situation much worse and your child may engage in behavior more difficult than what you started with. While teaching new behaviors is hard, nothing is more difficult than getting rid of maladaptive behaviors that have been practiced for years, behaviors that are sometimes allowed and sometimes not allowed without any rhyme or reason. Those are the most difficult to change.

I learned that, regardless of his cognitive level, Dustin's adaptive functioning skills would be crucial in increasing his independence and allowing him to make choices for his own life. Choice is so powerful. While it is ok to let my son express himself in the way that is most natural to him, if I never teach him the alternative, does he really have a choice? How many things in life will he never get to experience? One of the best "Bobbyisms" I have ever heard Dr. Newman say is, "It's better to be cool than brilliant." It's simple and so true. Who cares if my son can read, write, talk, add, and subtract if he still wears a diaper when there is not a medical reason why, or can't go to fairs, family functions, work or even his own chosen recreation because he is so disruptive?

Here we are 10 years later. Dustin is now 12 and still keeping his slow and steady pace. He has grown to be a sweet, affectionate boy. He was toilet trained by age 4 and a half. He can swim, he can ride a bike. He is amazing on the computer and can navigate the internet unbelievably well. He follows directions pretty well and can ask verbally, as well as via typing, for things that he needs and wants. He helps me shop at the store and puts groceries away. He dresses himself and is beginning to help with household chores. He interacts with his brother and sister and almost explodes with excitement on family trips, no matter how big or small the outing. None of this has been through luck. Every single skill has been carefully and consistently taught, one skill building on the other. But let's not sugarcoat it, there are challenges: over the years he has had periods of severe tantrums, when he would scream as if he were being murdered. His verbal ability is limited. We have had times of self-injury and aggression. He engages in pica, a behavior that involves eating or swallowing things that are not edible. He also will regurgitate food and play with it. He still makes noises and still, at times, engages in odd stereotypic movements.

I share this with you not to make you feel sorry for him, but to truly understand what he has been able to overcome. I want families to understand. Where there is a will, there is a way. Dustin, his school staff, and our family have worked and worked and worked to reduce these behaviors and increase his levels of independence. While these are behavior challenges, they are at such low levels there are slowly becoming a non-issue. His current ability to not be disruptive in public has been years in the making. Thousands of hours of practicing, hundreds of opportunities, sometimes literally blood, sweat, and tears, and all the while collecting data to help us know what was working and, if it wasn't, what we needed to change about our teaching to make it happen. We owe it to our son to try, but sometimes we do need a break. It can be very overwhelming; sometimes I know that we will not be able to follow through. It is important to recognize those days and know that it is okay. And on those days, don't even begin to try, because if you can not follow through, you may give in at the wrong time and make things worse than what you started with. Bobby also taught me this early on, and it has helped me tremendously, mentally and emotionally.

If it were not for the guidance I received from parents sharing their knowledge, if I did not take advantage of conferences by professionals in the field that are experts in autism, if we did not seek out private experienced behavior analysts and if Dustin did not receive true applied behavior analytic services implemented with fidelity, Jake would still be crying, "Mom, Dustin ruins everything!" Dustin is able to do things that we once only dreamed about. I have seen small miracles with him over the years and, oh my gosh how the quality of life for our family has improved. With each new skill, you can see the pride in his face. We have many great family memories and adventures and the pictures to prove it. I am thankful for all those who have supported us over the years and told me what things are possible and showed me how. While there are many challenges ahead, we are very hopeful for the future. We are very proud of Dustin. As he grows some things do get easier but again, nothing to do with "luck" – just constant, consistent, continuing moving forward with a purpose, never giving up.

(Bobby's note: I once had to follow Jennica to the podium. I was scheduled to deliver a paper after she did a presentation where she described a behavioral intervention she carried out to address some of Dustin's extreme tantrums. The function of the tantrums was not immediately obvious, and it was a complex functional analysis. Jennica showed vivid video and graphs detailing interventions as I watched audience members well up with tears and gasp as they watched, anxiously lean forward in their chairs – handkerchiefs and tissues were everywhere – and then breathe heavy sighs of relief when Jennica showed the behavior improving. She finished her talk and there was thunderous and sustained applause.

Then it was my turn to speak.

I got up to the podium, looked at my PowerPoint, looked out at the audience and said "Um . . . uh . . . I've got nothing here. Anybody want to get a sandwich?"

She did it to me again! We're done. I've gotta stop trying to follow her . . . or Lily . . . or Nicole . . . or . . .)

References and Suggested Reading

Ahearn, W. H., Castine, T., Nault, K., & Green, G. (2001). An assessment of food acceptance in children with autism or pervasive developmental disorder-not otherwise specified. *Journal of Autism and Developmental Disabilities, 31, 505-511.*

Ahearn, W. H., Clark, K. M., MacDonald, R. P. F., & Chung, B. I. (2007). Assessing and treating vocal stereotypy in children with autism. *Journal of Applied Behavior Analysis, 40,* 263-275.

American Psychiatric Association. (1994). *Diagnostic and statistical manual of mental disorders: 4th edition.* Washington, DC: Author.

Ashbaugh, R. & Peck, S. M. (1998). Treatment of sleep problems in a toddler: A replication of the faded bedtime with response cost protocol. *Journal of Applied Behavior Analysis, 31,* 127-129.

Athens, E. S., Vollmer, T. R., Sloman, K. N., & St. Peter Pipken, C. (2008). An analysis of vocal stereotypy and therapist fading. *Journal of Applied Behavior Analysis, 41,* 291-297.

Austin, J., & Carr, J. E. (2000). *Handbook of Applied Behavior Analysis.* Reno, NV: Context Press.

Azrin, N. H., & Foxx, R. M. (1971). A rapid method of toilet training the institutionalized retarded. *Journal of Applied Behavior Analysis, 4,* 89-99.

Bailey, J. S. & Burch, M. R. (2011). *Ethics for behavior analysts: 2nd expanded edition.* New York: Routledge.

Bailey, J. S. & Burch, M. (2006). *How to think like a behavior analyst.* Lawrence Erlbaum Associates, Inc.

Bach, R., & Moylan, J. J. (1975). Parents administered behavior therapy for inappropriate urination and encopresis: A case study. *Journal of Behavior Therapy and Experimental Psychiatry, 6,* 239-241.

Bettison, S. (1982). *Toilet training to independence for the handicapped: A manual for trainers.* Illinois: Charles C. Thomas.

Butler, J. F. (1977). Treatment of encopresis by overcorrection. *Psychological Reports, 40,* 639-646.

Carr, E. G., & Durand, V. M. (1985). Reducing behavior problems through functional communication training. *Journal of Applied Behavior Analysis, 18,* 111-26.

Cooper, J. O., Heron, T. E., & Heward, W. L. (1987). *Applied behavior analysis.* New Jersey: Prentice Hall.

Cooper, J. O., Heron, T. E., & Heward, W. L. (2007). *Applied Behavior Analysis.* Upper Saddle River, NJ: Pearson Education, Inc.

Crowley, C. P., & Armstrong, P. M. (1977). Positive practice, overcorrection and behavioral rehearsal in the treatment of three cases of encopresis. *Journal of Behavior Therapy and Experimental Psychiatry, 8,* 411-416.

Dunlap, G., Koegel, R. L., & Koegel, L. K. (1984). Continuity of treatment: Toilet training in multiple community settings. *Journal of the Association for the Severely Handicapped, 9,* 134-141.

Fisher, W. W., Adelinis, J. D., Thompson, R. H., Worsdell, A. S. & Zarcone, J. R. (1998). Functional analysis and treatment of destructive behavior maintained by termination of "don't" (and symmetrical "do") requests. *Journal of Applied Behavior Analysis, 31,* 339-356.

Frea, W. D., Koegel, R. L., & Koegel, L. K. (1993). *Understanding why problem behaviors occur: A guide for assisting parents in assessing causes of behavior and designing treatment plans.* Santa Barbara: University of California at Santa Barbara.

Glasberg, B. A. (2005). *Functional behavior assessment for people with autism: Making sense of seemingly senseless behavior*. Bethesda, MD: Woodbine House, Inc.

Glasberg, B. A. (2008). *Stop that seemingly senseless behavior!: FBA-based interventions for people with autism*. Bethesda, MD: Woodbine House, Inc.

Hanley, G. P., Iwata, B. A., & McCord, B. E. (2003). Functional analysis of problem behavior: A review. *Journal of Applied Behavior Analysis, 36,* 147-185.

Hanley, G. P., Piazza, C. C., Fisher, W. W., & Maglieri, K. A. (2005). On the effectiveness of and preference for punishment and extinction components of function-based interventions. *Journal of Applied Behavior Analysis, 38*, 51-65.

Horner, R. D., & Keilitz, I. (1975). Training mentally retarded adolescents to brush their teeth. *Journal of Applied Behavior Analysis, 8*, 301-309.

Johnson, B., & Cuvo, A. (1981). Teaching mentally retarded adults to cook. *Behavior Modification, 5,* 187-202.

Herndon, A. C., DiGuiseppi, C., Johnson, S. L., Leiferman, J., & Reynolds, A. (2009). Does nutritional intake differ between children with autism spectrum disorders and children with typical development? *Journal of Autism and Developmental Disorders, 39,* 212-222.

Gawley, E., Stephenson, K., Roane, H., Bouxsein, K., & Veenstra, R. (2011). *Self-monitoring and initiation in toileting training with a child with autism*. Munroe-Meyer Institute for Genetics and Rehabilitation.

Iwata, B. A., Pace, G. M., Dorsey, M. F., Zarcone, J. R., Vollmer, T. R., Smith, R. G., Rodgers, T. A., Lerman, D. C., Shore, B. A., Mazaleski, J. L., Goh, H. L., Cowdery, G. E., Kalsher, M. J., McCosh, K. C., & Willis, K. D. (1994). The functions of self-injurious behavior: An experimental epidemiological analysis. *Journal of Applied Behavior Analysis, 27,* 215-40.

Iwata, B. A., Dorsey, M. F., Slifer, K. J., Bauman, K. E., & Richman, G. S. (1994). Toward functional analysis of self-injury. *Journal of Applied Behavior Analysis, 27,* 197-209.

Kennedy, C. H., Meyer, K. A., Knowles, T., & Shukla, S. (2000). Analyzing the multiple functions of stereotypical behavior for students with autism: Implications for assessment and treatment. *Journal of Applied Behavior Analysis, 33,* 559-571.

Lovaas, O. I., Koegel, R., Simmons, J. Q., & Long, J. S. (1973). Some generalization and follow-up measures on autistic children in behavior therapy. *Journal of Applied Behavior Analysis, 6,* 131-166.

Liu-Gitz, L., & Banda, D. R. (2010). A replication of the RIRD strategy to decrease vocal stereotypy in a student with autism. *Behavioral Interventions, 25,* 77-87.

MacDonald, R., Green, G., Mansfield, R., Geckeler, A., Gardenier, N., Anderson, J., Holcomb, W., & Sanchez, J. (2007). Stereotypy in young children with autism and typically developing children. *Research in Developmental Disabilities, 28,* 266-277.

Matson, J. L., Kiely, S. L., & Bamburg, J. W. (1997). The effect of stereotypies on adaptive skills as assessed with the DASH-II and Vineland Adaptive Behavior Scales. *Research in Developmental Disabilities, 18,* 471-476.

Neef, N. A., & Peterson, S. M. (2007). Functional behavior assessment. In J. O. Cooper, T. E. Heron, & W. L. Heward (Eds.), *Applied Behavior Analysis* (pp. 500-524). Upper Saddle River, NJ: Pearson Education, Inc.

Newman, B. (2011). *Gentle redirection of aggressive and destructive behavior (GRAD).* Manual to accompany training.

O'Brien, S., Ross, L. V., & Christophersen, E. R. (1986). Primary encopresis: Evaluation and treatment. *Journal of Applied Behavior Analysis, 19,* 137-145.

Piazza, C. C. & Fisher, W. (1991). A faded bedtime with response cost protocol for treatment of multiple sleep problems in children. *Journal of Applied Behavior Analysis, 24,* 129-140.

Premack, D. (1959). Toward empirical behavior laws I: Positive reinforcement. *Psychological Review, 66*, 219-233.

Shabani, D., Katz, R., Wilder, D., Beauchamp, K., Taylor, C., & Fischer, K. (2002). Increasing social initiations in children with autism: Effects of a tactile prompt. *Journal of Applied Behavior Analysis, 35*, 79-83.

Shepherd, L. A. M. (2010). The effects of response interruption and contingent demands on reducing vocal stereotypy in young children with autism spectrum disorder. *Unpublished Master's Thesis.* The Ohio State University, Columbus, OH.

Shore, B. A., Iwata, B. A., DeLeon, I. G., Kahng, S., & Smith, R. G. (1997). An analysis of reinforcer substitutability using object manipulation and self-injury as competing responses. *Journal of Applied Behavior Analysis, 30,* 21-41.

Smith, E. A., & Van Houten, R. (1996). A comparison of the characteristics of self-stimulatory behaviors in normal children and children with developmental delays. *Research in Developmental Disabilities, 17,* 254-268.

Smith, L., Smith, P., & Lee, S. K. (2000). Behavioural treatment of urinary incontinence and encopresis in children with learning disabilities: Transfer of stimulus control. *Developmental Medicine and Child Neurology, 42*, 276.

Sokol, R.I., Webster, K.L., Thompson, N.S. & Stevens, D.A. (2005) Whining as mother-directed speech. *Infant and Child and Development, 14*, 478-490.

Tarbox, J., Schiff, A, & Najdowski, A. C. (2010). Parent-implemented procedural modification of escape extinction in the treatment of food selectivity in a young child with autism. *Education and Treatment of Children, 33,* 223-234.

Thinesen, P., & Bryan, A. (1981). The use of sequential picture cues in the initiation and maintenance of grooming behaviors with mentally retarded adults. *Mental Retardation, 19*, 246-250.

Vollmer, T. R. (1994). The concept of automatic reinforcement: Implications for behavioral research in developmental disabilities. *Research in Developmental Disabilities, 15,* 187-297.

About the Authors

Patrick Bardsley received his bachelors degree with honors in Sociology from the University of Birmingham, England. Presently, he is matriculated at Long Island University, CW Post Graduate School of Education in the Special Needs CASE Program and a candidate for his Master's degree in 2012. In addition, he is working on his coursework towards his BCBA. For the past 6 years, Patrick has worked directly with individuals with autism and related conditions, for 3 of those serving as a supervisory co-coordinator at a special needs summer camp program. Currently, he is co-founder and program director of Spectrum Designs Foundation and the Nicholas Center for Autism both based in Port Washington, New York.

Cristiane B. Souza Bertone, MSEd, BCBA, is a board certified behavior analyst and a certified special education teacher. She works as an educator, behavior consultant, and expert witness for individuals diagnosed with developmental disabilities. She provides behaviorally-based interventions for individuals ages 1 and older around the tri-state area and internationally. She develops and presents research related to autism and maladaptive behaviors, and develops and presents training workshops for families and professionals. She sits on the board of directors for Manos Unidas, a non-profit organization servicing individuals with various disabilities in Peru.

Alexandra Brown works as a Program Supervisor at the Lizard Children's Centre, Sydney, Australia. She is a registered Psychologist in NSW. Alex studied at the Australian College of Applied Psychology, after completing a Bachelor of Psychology at the University of Wollongong. She has been working with children with autism and related disorders, and their families, for the past ten years.

Michelle Furminger is a Board Certified Assistant Behavior Analyst and is currently a Program Supervisor at the Lizard Centre in Sydney, Australia. This centre is an early intervention clinic specializing in ABA programs for children with autism. She has been in the field since 1998 and has a special interest in toileting behavior. She has taken her love and interest in this field around Australia presenting workshops on the "poo" topic. She also presented a paper at the Phoenix ABAI in 2009 on her beloved topic as well.

Alayna T. Haberlin, PhD, BCBA, grew up in the San Francisco Bay Area. She went to the University of Nevada, Reno, to get her BA in Psychology and Spanish, and snowboard in Lake Tahoe. Somewhere between the slopes and the library, the ABA bug bit her. Alayna continued her studies in ABA by getting her MA in Psychology at the University of the Pacific. The thirst for knowledge was not satisfied with a Master's, so she went to The Ohio State University and got her PhD in Special Education and ABA. Not only did she start to quench her thirst for ABA but she was unexpectedly exposed to the Buckeye Nation. Go Bucks! After spending a few cold winters in Ohio, she relocated to sunny Sydney, Australia, where she works at the Lizard Centre.

Sheila Jodlowski has been working with children with autism spectrum disorders for more than 15 years. She received her doctorate in Applied Behavior Analysis from Teachers College Columbia University. Sheila is adjunct faculty at Manhattanville College in Purchase, NY, where she teaches Behavior Analysis. She provides academic and behavioral consulting services for families in the Mid-Hudson Valley region of New York. In 2009, Sheila founded Hudson Valley Behavioral Solutions (HVBS) in Duchess County, New York, providing individual and group services for children and families. All services at HVBS are delivered using behavior analytic approaches—from consultation to individual instruction to social skills classes. Sheila is a regular presenter at national conferences on behavior analysis.

Susan Kenny is a proud mom of three beautiful, energetic children and blessed by her loving husband, Tom. After graduating from Dowling College with a BA in Elementary Education, Susan moved on to secure a Masters in Literacy Education from Dowling College and a certification as a School District Leader from the College of Saint Rose, Albany. Susan has worked in the field of education for over 15 years. Starting her career as an elementary teacher and reading specialist, Susan was always eager to create learning environments for students with different abilities that allowed these students to interact with typical peers and be true members of their school community. When Susan transitioned from teaching to administration, she was faced with many challenges that would later serve as examples of changing school culture and perception about educating children with different abilities. Several of these examples are presented in this book. These experiences have influenced many educators to re-think how they approach and interact with children that have different abilities. Being reflective of practices and setting high, obtainable expectations for all students with special needs is embedded in her daily interactions with students and their families.

Cassie le Fevre, MPsych(Clin), is a psychologist with 15 years experience working with children with autism spectrum disorders. After being introduced to ABA and all its benefits, she travelled to the San Francisco Bay Area to complete an internship with Behavior Analysts, Inc., under the supervision of Jim Partington, PhD, BCBA-D, Mark Sundberg, PhD, BCBA-D, and Mary Ann Powers, BCBA-D. She spent four years in Sydney, Australia, working as a Program Supervisor at the Lizard Children's Centre before returning to her hometown of Hobart, Tasmania, to be close to family. When she is not tap dancing or learning to speak Greek, Cassie is completing the requirements to sit for the BCBA exam.

Ana C. Madeira, MSED, has been working with children with autism spectrum disorders for over six years. She has worked as a teacher in school settings, as well as providing in-home Early Intervention services, and ABA to children and families. She received her Bachelor of Arts in Psychology from The College of New Rochelle, and her Master of Science in Early Childhood and Special Education from The College of New Rochelle.

Elizabeth McAllister, BSc, MSc, BCBA, lives in Hamilton, Ontario, Canada. She currently works as a behavior analyst for children with ASD and passed the BCBA exam during the preparation of this book!

Jennica Nill is a wife and mother of 3. Since her son was diagnosed with autism in 2001, she had dedicated herself to becoming an educated consumer and has attended over 400 hours of workshops related to treatment of severe problem behavior, applied behavior analysis and special education advocacy. She is a 2004 New York State Partners in Policymaking Graduate. Since 2005, she has been serving as consumer representative to the Board of Directors of the Behavior Analyst Certification Board (BACB). In 2007, Jennica completed the Special Education Advocacy Training (SEAT project) through the Council of Parent Attorneys and Advocates. Currently, she serves on the board for the ELIJA Foundation and the legislative committee for the New York State Association for Behavior Analysis. Jennica is currently working as a special education advocate at the Long Island Advocacy Center, a not-for-profit organization dedicated to protecting the legal rights of students and individuals with disabilities.

Bobby Newman is a Board Certified Behavior Analyst and Licensed Psychologist. Bobby was first author on nine previous book projects and has authored over two dozen articles. He provides staff training and consultation around the world, and has been honored for this work by several parents' groups, including having an award named in his honor by Families for Effective Autism Treatment of Central New York and being knighted by the F.A.I.T.H. group of England. Despite this, Sir Robert prefers his humble role of Dark Overlord of ABA, the stage persona he developed to keep people awake during lengthy presentations of sometimes technical material. In 2011, Bobby completed his first three marathons. When they make the movie of his life, he does not want to be played by Woody Harrelson.

David M. Newman is currently in fifth grade. He loves to act in musical theater, from which he drew his inspiration to write his play. He loves his family and the beach, and enjoys running, swimming, playing soccer, and playing piano and bass clarinet. He is affectionately known as the "World's Best Peer Model."

Lauren Porter has a Masters Degree in School Psychology from St. John's University. She currently works at the East Quogue School and St. Joseph's College on Long Island.

Gail Quinn, BCaBA, lives and works in beautiful Sydney, Australia with the pediatric clinic, Lizard Children's Centre. "Lizard" is one of Australia's leading providers of evidence based intervention for young children with autism and related disorders. Gail has been the Associate Director since January of 2011 and also serves as Program Supervisor. Married to an Ozzie, she has been continent hopping with her husband for the past decade. Prior to this appointment, she spent several years in the United States working with the Lovaas Institute Midwest under the clinical direction of Eric V. Larsson, Ph.D., BCBA, digging herself out of snow drifts 5 months of the year in her home state of Minnesota.

Dana Reinecke is a Board Certified Behavior Analyst. She earned her doctorate in Learning Processes and Behavior Analysis Psychology from the Graduate Center of the City University of New York. Dana is the Department Chair of the Center for Applied Behavior Analysis (CABA) for the Sage Colleges. CABA is composed of two highly-regarded online graduate programs for the training of potential board certified behavior analysts. Dana also designed the newly-launched Achieve Degree for the Sage Colleges. The Achieve Degree is a fully online Bachelor's degree program for students with autism and other disabilities who are academically capable, but find a traditional college experience challenging. Dana provides consultation in behavior analysis to schools, school districts, and families of children with disabilities. She has co-authored books and book chapters in behavior analysis and autism, and published research in peer-reviewed journals. Dana has presented workshops and research at local, national, and international conferences. She has also provided training and consultation in Mexico, Ireland, and Australia. Dana is currently conducting research on effective on-line learning and using technology to teach individuals with autism. Dana lives in Long Beach, NY, with her very talented husband and her even more talented son.

Allison Roberts received her Bachelor of Arts in Psychology and Early Childhood from Queens College and a Master's of Science in Education from Hofstra University. She has been teaching for the past 15 years in both a school setting as well as in homes. Allison was the recipient of the NYSABA Direct Service Provider Award.

Lillianna Rogers is twelve years old and lives in Baldwinsville, NY. She is the oldest of three children. Her brothers are Joey and Matt. Her brother Joey has autism. Lillianna and her family founded Families for Effective Autism Treatment of Central New York. She considers herself an ambassador for all brothers and sisters of kids with autism. Her goals include teaching other kids about autism. Every year she presents information to her class about autism. She believes that siblings are great friends and teachers and that the whole family should act like a team.

Nicole Rogerson is the Managing Director of the Lizard Children's Centre. She lives in Sydney with her husband and 2 sons. Nicole left a career in Marketing and Public Relations in 1999 when her son was diagnosed with autism. In 2003 she joined with Speech Pathologist and Behavioral Clinician, Elizabeth Watson, to establish the Lizard Children's Centre, which provides evidence-based intensive early intervention programs for children with autism and developmental delays. Nicole is the founding Director and CEO of Autism Awareness, which she set up in 2007 in order to increase awareness of autism in the wider Australian community. Nicole is a frequent public speaker on ASD and facilitates a number of educational seminars around the country. She sat on the Federal Government's Autism Advisory Board prior to the introduction of the Helping Children with Autism funding package, and continues to work for better access to and government support for evidence-based intensive early intervention programs for children with autism. Nicole and her colleague, Dr. James Morton, were the instigators of the 1000 hours campaign in 2009 and this year, Nicole hosted the inaugural Australian National Autism Summit. In June 2011, Nicole was asked to present on the work of Autism Awareness at the United Nations in New York.

Leigh Ann M. Shepherd, M.A., BCBA, has spent nearly ten years working with children on the autism spectrum. She is currently Co-Director and one of the founders of Central Ohio Behavioral Consulting, LLC. COBC commits itself to helping families overcome daily challenges that often exist when raising a child diagnosed with an autism spectrum disorder and offering the same type of service to children with other special needs. She previously spent over eight years at Nationwide Children's Hospital Center for Autism Spectrum Disorders. Leigh Ann holds her Master of Arts degree in Special Education/Applied Behavior Analysis and is Board Certified in Behavior Analysis. Leigh

Ann is married to her wonderful and supportive husband, Patrick. They have two young daughters and live in Marysville, Ohio.

Melissa Slobin, MA, CCC-SLP, earned her degree in speech-language pathology at New York University and she is currently enrolled in the BCBA program at Hunter College. She works with children and young adults who are diagnosed with a variety of communication disorders, including autism spectrum disorders. Melissa and her husband Gary recently ran their first marathon while raising funds for Autism Speaks. They attempt to set philanthropic examples for their 3 daughters, Jacqueline, Maya, and Rebecca. Melissa would especially like to thank Dr. Newman for clarifying all of her prior misconceptions of Applied Behavior Analysis and teaching her interesting phrases like "technicolor yawn."

Stella L. Spanakos, MA, retired after 13 years of teaching High School Social Studies on Long Island and English as a Second Language at the Universita di Bari, Faculta di Economia e Commercia, Bari, Italy, to work full time with her son Nicholas who has autism. In 1994 Ms. Spanakos started a Holiday Shopping Party at the Polo Ralph Lauren Store, Americana Manhasset location, to raise funds for the Manhasset Auxiliary of the AHRC; which led to her brainchild, Champions for Charity, established by the Americana Manhasset in 1996. Since its inception Champions for Charity has raised nearly six million dollars for over 90 not-for-profit organizations. The Manhasset Public School District and the Manhasset Parent Association for Special Education (PASE) honored Ms. Spanakos in May 2009 for eight years of leadership as president of Manhasset PASE. She has been a parent member and an educational advocate for the past 15 years. She is a member of the Molloy College Special and Inclusive Education Advisory Board and guest lectures at their Graduate School of Special Education. Ms. Spanakos has served as Vice President of the Board of Trustees for the ELIJA School, and was awarded the ELIJA Foundation Parent Award in 2007 for Contribution to the

Autism Community. Stella is a member of the Council for Exceptional Learners, New York State Association for Applied Behavior Analysis (NYSABA), and the Long Island Task Force on Aging Out, and the USTA, because what is the purpose of life without tennis? Ms. Spanakos is co-founder and CEO of the Nicholas Center for Autism, and Spectrum Designs Foundation Ltd., located in Port Washington, NY. The Nicholas Center for Autism (NCFA) offers a variety of services, geared toward improving the lives of young men and women with autism and similar conditions. Spectrum Designs Foundation is a not-for-profit business founded to employ people on the spectrum in a supported work environment. www.spectrumdesigns.org. Other publications include contributions to: Sabatelli, Antonia Orsi. (1984). Nuovo Testo Di Traduzioni Per Esercitazioni. Bari, Italy: Cacucci Editore. I would like to thank Bobby and Dana for this opportunity and for giving new meaning to the cult classic *The Rocky Horror Picture Show*.

Lisa M. Swift, MA, SBL, BCBA is a Board Certified Behavior Analyst. She received her Master of Arts degree from Teacher's College, Columbia University in Behavior Disorders. Lisa has worked as a special educator in Westchester, NY, for 10 years and also works privately with clients and their families in the NY metro area. She has conducted workshops and presented research at national and international conferences.

Sibel Tenish has a degree in psychology from the Macquarie University, as well as a Master in Health Science (Behavioral Science) from Sydney University. Currently, Sibel is working as a Program Supervisor at the Lizard Centre in Sydney and is looking forward to completing her psychology internship in May 2012. Sibel has worked with children who have autism and other related disorders for almost 9 years. She has also provided therapy for children who were travelling in beautiful Rome, Italy, and the gorgeous Hamilton Island, a popular island resort on the east coast of Australia. In addition to travelling, Sibel especially enjoys the challenges of working with very active children. She is so passionate about ABA that she is often applying the basic principles of reinforcement and extinction to her family and friends!

Edward Vinski earned a PhD in Educational Psychology from the Graduate School and University Center of CUNY, a MS in School Psychology from St. John's University, and a BA in Psychology from Providence College. He is currently an Assistant Professor of Education at St. Joseph's College and a School Psychologist at East Quogue School. When not bringing balance to the Force, he tries to be a writer and educator on Long Island where he lives with his family.

10909187R00098

Made in the USA
Charleston, SC
15 January 2012